I/O Applications Workbook

Industrial/Organizational Psychology
An Applied Approach

SIXTH EDITION

Michael G. Aamodt
Radford University

Prepared by

Michael G. Aamodt
Radford University

WADSWORTH
CENGAGE Learning™

Australia • Brazil • Japan • Korea • Mexico • Singapore • Spain • United Kingdom • United States

WADSWORTH
CENGAGE Learning

© 2010 Wadsworth, Cengage Learning

ALL RIGHTS RESERVED. No part of this work covered by the copyright herein may be reproduced, transmitted, stored, or used in any form or by any means graphic, electronic, or mechanical, including but not limited to photocopying, recording, scanning, digitizing, taping, Web distribution, information networks, or information storage and retrieval systems, except as permitted under Section 107 or 108 of the 1976 United States Copyright Act, without the prior written permission of the publisher.

For product information and technology assistance, contact us at
**Cengage Learning Customer & Sales Support,
1-800-354-9706**

For permission to use material from this text or product, submit all requests online at **www.cengage.com/permissions**
Further permissions questions can be emailed to
permissionrequest@cengage.com

ISBN-13: 978-0-495-60371-9
ISBN-10: 0-495-60371-6

Wadsworth
10 Davis Drive
Belmont, CA 94002-3098
USA

Cengage Learning is a leading provider of customized learning solutions with office locations around the globe, including Singapore, the United Kingdom, Australia, Mexico, Brazil, and Japan. Locate your local office at: **international.cengage.com/region**

Cengage Learning products are represented in Canada by Nelson Education, Ltd.

For your course and learning solutions, visit
academic.cengage.com

Purchase any of our products at your local college store or at our preferred online store
www.ichapters.com

Printed in the United States of America
1 2 3 4 5 6 7 12 11 10 09

Contents

1.1	Research designs	1
1.2	Designing a study	5
1.3	Reviewing research articles	6
2.1	Critiquing job descriptions	8
2.2	Writing a job description	10
2.3	Identifying KSAOs	11
2.4	The critical incident technique	13
2.5	Designing a job evaluation system	23
2.6	Determining pay equity	27
3.1	Federally protected classes	29
3.2	Determining adverse impact	30
3.3	Responses to adverse impact	31
3.4	Legality of employment practices	32
3.5	Sexual harassment	33
3.6	Understanding affirmative action	34
3.7	Employee privacy issues	35
3.8	Testing your legal knowledge	36
4.1	Reading help-wanted ads	37
4.2	Writing help-wanted ads	38
4.3	Point of purchase recruitment	39
4.4	Employee recruitment	40
4.5	Identifying KSAOs	41
4.6	Developing interview questions	42
4.7	Scoring interview questions	47
4.8	Finding career resources	49
4.9	Surviving the employment interview	50
4.10	Resume writing	51
4.11	Classroom exercise: Scoring a structured interview	53
5.1	Trait approach	58
5.2	Cognitive ability	59
5.3	Leaderless group discussion	61
5.4	Personality inventories	64
5.5	Interest inventories	71
5.6	Integrity testing	77
5.7	Resume evaluation	79
6.1	Locating test information	81
6.2	Using the utility formula and tables	83
6.3	Determining the proportion of correct decisions	85
6.4	Using banding to reduce adverse impact	87
7.1	360-degree feedback	89
7.2	Creating performance dimensions	90
7.3	Paired-comparison technique	91
7.4	Writing behavioral statements	92
7.5	Evaluating employee performance	93
7.6	Rating errors	94
7.7	Performance appraisal interviews	95

8.1	Needs assessment: Task analysis	97
8.2	Needs assessment: Person analysis	99
8.3	Evaluating training programs: 1	101
8.4	Evaluating training programs: 2	103
9.1	Focused free-write: Motivation	105
9.2	Self-esteem	106
9.3	Intrinsic versus extrinsic motivation	108
9.4	Goal setting	111
9.5	Reinforcement hierarchy	112
9.6	Expectancy and equity theories	113
9.7	Motivation case study	114
9.8	Your own motivation theory	115
10.1	Focused free-write — Satisfaction	117
10.2	Stability of job satisfaction	118
10.3	Core self-evaluation	119
10.4	Your level of life satisfaction	121
10.5	Case study	123
10.6	Absenteeism	124
11.1	Focused free-write	125
11.2	Horizontal communication	126
11.3	Nonverbal communication	127
11.4	Communication overload	130
11.5	Your listening style	131
11.6	Listening styles	132
11.7	Listening quiz	133
11.8	Readability	136
12.1	Thinking about leadership	137
12.2	Understanding your leadership style	138
13.1	Focused free-write: Group dynamics	145
13.2	Increasing group membership	146
13.3	Teams	147
13.4	Competition and conflict	148
13.5	Cohen Conflict Response Inventory (short version)	149
13.6	Reactions to conflict	151
13.7	Reacting to conflict	152
14.1	Sacred cow hunts	155
14.2	Acceptance of change	156
14.3	Organizational culture	157
14.4	Vroom-Yetton decision-making model	158
14.5	Downsizing	160
14.6	Work schedules	161
15.1	Type A behavior	163
15.2	Optimism	165
15.3	Lifestyle questionnaire	167
15.4	Empowering and motivating yourself	169

Exercise 1.1
Research Designs

In each of the following examples, determine the type of research design used (experiment, quasi-experiment, survey, correlation, archival, meta-analysis) and then identify the independent variables and the dependent variables (if any). Also identify any problems with the study and offer some suggestions for improvement.

A. A human resource manager was interested in determining if there was a relationship between employee satisfaction and performance. The HR manager had 800 employees complete a job satisfaction inventory and then compared the scores on this inventory with supervisor's ratings of job performance.

Type of study _____

Independent variable _____

Dependent variable _____

Problems and Suggestions

_____

_____

_____

_____

B. A study was conducted to determine if men and women were being paid equitably at Acme Manufacturing. To test this question, company payroll records were examined to compare the average salaries of male and female employees. The results indicated that the average man earned $32,176 per year whereas the average woman earned $30,100.

Type of study _____

Independent variable _____

Dependent variable _____

Problems and Suggestions

_____

_____

_____

_____

C. A supervisor noticed that absenteeism was higher on the Tuesday following a Monday Night Football game than on other days. To test her idea, she counted the number of days her employees missed on Tuesdays not following a football game and compared them with the number of days missed on the Tuesdays following a football game. She found that the absenteeism rate was 12% on "regular" Tuesdays and 20% on Tuesdays following a football game.

Type of study _____

Independent variable _____

Dependent variable _____

Problems and suggestions

_____

_____

_____

_____

_____

D. Prior to developing an on-site child-care center, Community General Hospital wanted to ensure that enough of its employees would use the center. Amanda Blake, the nursing supervisor, sent a questionnaire to the hospital's employees asking them if they would use the center, and how much they would be willing to pay per week for on-site child care.

Type of study _____

Independent variable _____

Dependent variable _____

Problems and suggestions

_____

_____

_____

_____

_____

_____

E. A professor was interested in discovering the effect of incentives on employee performance. He went back through every issue of the *Journal of Applied Psychology* and the *Journal of Management* and statistically combined the results reported in all of the relevant articles. The mean effect size (d) of .63 indicated that incentives did increase employee performance.

Type of study _____

Independent variable _____

Dependent variable _____

Problems and suggestions

_____

_____

_____

_____

_____

_____

F. A manager worried that her employees were not happy with the organization. To confirm her fears, she had each of her employees provide written answers to 10 questions about their attitudes toward work. She was surprised to find that her employees were happier than she thought.

Type of study _____

Independent variable _____

Dependent variable _____

Problems and Suggestions

_____

_____

_____

_____

_____

G. A police chief was considering the requirement that all new officers must have a college degree. Before doing this, however, he went into the files and looked at the education level of his current officers and compared their education with their police performance. He discovered that officers with college degrees performed better than their less educated peers.

Type of study _____

Independent variable _____

Dependent variable _____

Problems and suggestions

_____

_____

_____

_____

_____

H. A professor hypothesized that people could be trained to detect deception in employment interviews. To test her hypothesis, 50 students were given training on detecting deception and 50 students were given training on interpersonal skills. The 100 students then viewed one of two interviews, one with a person lying and the other with a person telling the truth. After viewing the tape, the students were asked to indicate whether the applicant in the tape was telling the truth about her work history. The professor found that the students who were trained to detect deception were no more accurate than the other students.

Type of study _____

Independent variable _____

Dependent variable _____

Problems and suggestions

_____

_____

_____

_____

_____

Exercise 1.2
Designing a Study

You are the human resource director for a company of 10,000 employees specializing in the production of swimming products. Due to the increased complexity of the manufacturing process, you are interested in improving the basic skills (e.g., math, reading, writing) of your employees. Two methods look promising—one involving interactive video and the other involving the use of workbooks. The interactive video approach would cost about $500,000 and the workbooks about $200,000.

Design a study to help you make a decision. Describe your sample and your research method. How would you arrive at a conclusion about what to do?

Exercise 1.3
Reviewing Research Articles

On the following page is a short summary of a hypothetical study published in a journal. Read the study and discuss any problems you find with the way in which the study was conducted, the author's conclusions, or the way in which the article was written.

Effect of Smoking on Management Performance

Winston Butts
Vantage University

In recent years, many organizations have implemented programs to encourage employees to stop smoking (Ash, 1971). This movement toward decreasing smoking in the workplace is an attempt to reduce health care costs as well as satisfy the rights of nonsmokers (Butts, 1975).

However, research on the effects of these programs is mixed. Whereas some studies support the idea of financial savings (e.g., Stogie, 1970), others have shown no improvements in employee health or increases in organizational profits. Because of this lack of consistency, it is the purpose of the present study to determine if smoking might actually increase performance.

Method

Participants

The participants in the study were 15 managers employed by a large manufacturer of munitions and blasting caps. Eight of the managers smoked at work, and seven of the managers were nonsmokers. Ten of the managers were women and five were men. The mean age of the managers was 36.3, with the youngest being 21 and the oldest 65.

Procedure

The experimenter spent 10 days at the organization observing the 15 managers. Each time a manager did something right, he was given a point. Each time a manager did something wrong, a point was deducted. At the end of the 10 days, a manager's performance was determined by his total number of points.

Results and Discussion

The managers' performance scores were correlated with their smoking status. The results of this analysis indicated a correlation coefficient of .20. Though the correlation coefficient was not statistically significant, it was in the predicted direction. In other words, managers who smoked performed better than those who did not. Thus, the results of this study indicate that smoking causes better managerial performance.

One reason for this finding might be that smoking allows a manager to calm down when he is anxious, thus resulting in better performance (Puffer, 1971). Another reason might be that smoking is a sign of status and maturity (Burns, 1978) and good managers smoke to enhance their image. On the basis of the results of this study, organizations should either hire managers who smoke or get their nonsmoking managers to start smoking.

Exercise 2.1
Critiquing Job Descriptions

The purpose of this exercise is to familiarize you with the correct form for the various parts of a job description. On the next two pages, you will find a job description that contains several errors. Circle the errors and indicate why they are problems.

Restaurant Associate
Nora's Diner

Job Summary

The Restaurant Associate is responsible for performing a variety of tasks involved in the preparation and sales of food. Duties include preparing food, cooking food, taking customer orders, and cleaning the restaurant.

Work Activities

Food Preparation
- Remove buns from boxes and place on food preparation table
- Takes meat and chicken from the freezer and places on table to thaw
- Takes condiments from the refrigerator and places them on food preparation table
- Inspect meat and chicken to make sure they are safe to eat
- Handle problems

Cooking
- Place fries and breaded fish patties into vat and remove when high-pitched alarm goes off
- Cooks hamburgers, chicken, and hot dogs on the grill
- Puts grilled food onto bun and adds requested condiments

Cleaning
- Wipes counter and tables as needed
- Cleans the grill at the end of each shift
- Changes cooking oil when the bottom of the vat can't be seen or after several customer complaints
- Uses RK-9 to clean tables after manager indicates a 10-6 has occurred
- Mops
- Cleans cooking utensils at end of shift
- Sweeps and cleans parking lot area

Tools and Equipment Used
- Deep-fat fryer
- Grill
- Cleaning materials (e.g., mop, rags, cleanser)
- Cash register
- Common cooking utensils (e.g., spatulas, tongs)

Materials and Substances Exposed To
- RK-9
- Wesson cooking oil
- Meat, poultry, chicken, fish, potatoes, bread
- Draino

Job Context

The Restaurant Associate works an 8-hour shift, 5 days per week. The actual days and times worked vary based on a rotating schedule. Psychological stress is high when the restaurant is busy or customers get angry. Physical stress is moderate as the Restaurant Associate spends all 8 hours standing, with extensive bending and leaning. At times, crates weighing 80 pounds must be lifted.

Performance Appraisal

The Restaurant Associate is evaluated each month on the standard Nora's Diner performance appraisal instrument. Bonuses can be earned by having few customer complaints, no shrinkage, and no citations for health or safety violations.

Competencies

Upon Hire
- ability to count change back to customers
- no mental or physical problems
- must be bondable
- excellent communication skills
- be flexible

After Hire
- Knowledge of restaurant menu and recipes
- Knowledge of restaurant policies

Exercise 2.2
Writing a Job Description

In Chapter 2, you learned how to write a job description. This exercise will give you a chance to apply that knowledge. To complete this exercise:

1) Pair up with another person in your class.

2) Take turns interviewing each other about jobs that each of you currently has or had at one time.

3) Use the information from the interviews to write a job description similar to that found in your text on pages 40-42.

4) You will probably want to type your job description so that it looks professional.

Notes:

Exercise 2.3
Identifying KSAOs

Part A. For each of the following characteristics, indicate whether the characteristic is a knowledge, skill, ability, or other characteristic. Some of these might fall under more than one category.

1. Typing speed   _____

2. Finger dexterity   _____

3. Driving a car   _____

4. Traffic rules   _____

5. A driver's license   _____

6. A friendly personality   _____

7. Ten years of experience   _____

8. Basic intelligence   _____

9. Physical strength   _____

10. Color vision   _____

11. Being a nonsmoker   _____

12. Customer service experience _____

13. Use of PowerPoint   _____

14. Willingness to work weekends _____

15. Spelling and grammar   _____

16. Writing reports   _____

Part B. For each of the following tasks, list the KSAOs needed to successfully perform the task. Sample KSAOs can be found in the O*Net comparison chart on the text website (http://www.thomsonedu.com/psychology/aamodt).

Task   KSAOs

1. Pulling a citizen from a burning vehicle   _____

2. Driving a patrol car in pursuit of motorists   _____

   _____

3. Writing traffic citations to motorists who violate   _____
   traffic regulations
   _____

4. Chasing suspects on foot   _____

   _____

5. Determining the cause of an automobile accident   _____

   _____

6. Testifying in court   _____

   _____

7. Providing a lost motorist with directions   _____

   _____

8. Searching a car for weapons or evidence   _____

   _____

12

Exercise 2.4
The Critical Incident Technique

In Chapter 2 you learned about the critical incident technique. This exercise will give you a chance to actually conduct a job analysis using the critical incident technique. On the following pages are critical incidents written for restaurant server positions. To complete this exercise:

1) Cut out each of the critical incidents (the pages are intentionally one-sided so make it easier to ut out the incidents)
2) Sort the incidents into piles of similar incidents.
3) Name each pile.
4) Count the number of incidents in each pile (any incident number beginning with a "P" is an example of poor performance, and any incident beginning with a "G" is an example of good performance).
5) Enter your dimensions (names of your piles) and the number of incidents into the chart below.

Dimension	Poor Performance	Good Performance	Total
1.			
2.			
3.			
4.			
5.			
6.			
7.			
8.			
9.			
10.			
11.			

Critical Incidents of Poor Performance

P01 My bill was $5.76, so I gave the server $10.01. When he brought back my change, he gave me four ones, two dimes, and five pennies. The idiot didn't realize that I gave him the penny because I wanted a quarter, not a bunch of change!

P02 My waitress brought me a sandwich, and it was cold. I asked her if she could take it back and microwave it to warm it up. She said that the deli sandwiches are supposed to be cold. I told her that I still wanted mine warm, and she said she couldn't do it.

P03 She brought me a glass of tea and never once asked if I wanted a refill.

P04 I asked for a sandwich without mayonnaise and asked the waiter if he would substitute BBQ sauce for the mayonnaise. He said he would have to charge me 25 cents extra. What kind of poor customer service is that anyway?

P05 We were at a restaurant, and the waitress brought us our food. We never saw her again until it was time to get the bill.

P06 Once I was at a restaurant and it took over 10 minutes for the waiter to come to the table.

P07 I was at a restaurant and the waitress walked by and dropped salsa on the floor. It splattered all over me.

P08 The server approached us with a negative attitude from the minute we got there. It was as if he were trying to pick a fight.

P09 We were seated at a table 15 minutes before the waitress even showed up at our table. Then she disappeared for another 20 minutes before returning. The sad part was that the restaurant wasn't even busy.

P10 The waitress served our food to the table behind us and served us their food. The cook made our food again. This time she put it in a to-go box and gave it to her friends. Finally, on the third try we got our own food, but by that time we had already missed our movie.

P11 The waitress brought food out for each person about 5 minutes apart. Even then, she got the orders wrong.

P12 We sat for 20 minutes before the waiter came and then another 10 minutes before having our orders taken.

P13 We went to this restaurant and placed an order. We had an appetizer and sat around for awhile to wait for our dinner. After about an hour we began to ask what was going on. It seems as though our waitress took our order and went home for the night.

P14 The waitress never returned to our table to check on how we were doing.

P15 The waiter never asked if we needed refills for our drinks. We got his attention by yelling at him.

P16 When going out to dinner with a large group after a basketball game, a group of 10 kids were at one table and their parents at another. The parents were given prompt service and the kids received their dinner an hour after the parents received theirs. The kids' table never received drinks with the meal. The bill came to over $120, and the server was not given a tip.

P17 A server at this restaurant spilled nachos on us.

P18 At this restaurant there was muck in my glass of wine. The server told us that he was having a food fight with the cook in the kitchen.

P19 The server just let all the dirty dishes pile up on our table. We had dishes from our appetizers, salads, and meals. We could barely move!

P20 This waiter kept trying to make idle conversation. My date and I were trying to talk and we really didn't want to chit-chat with the waiter.

P21 Once I asked for salad dressing and the waitress finally came back 30 minutes later with my salad dressing — after I had already finished eating.

P22 The worst server I ever had was this guy who was never around. We had to ask other servers for our needs.

P23 We arrived at the restaurant 45 minutes before they were to close. The waiter was very upset because he wanted to go home, so he mixed up our orders. When we complained he refused to take our orders back.

P24 It was a very slow night, and the wait staff was preoccupied with personal discussions. We waited a long time before we left without eating.

P25 After my family and I had eaten, my daughter ordered dessert. When the waiter brought the dessert, it slid off the tray and into my lap.

P26 I ordered a steak cooked medium, and it came out all red. I told the waiter that there was a problem and he got all upset. He tried to tell me that a medium steak should be red. I told him that I had no intention of becoming a cannibal, so take the steak back.

P27 I was seated at this pizza place and waited for someone to take my order. Finally someone showed up and took my order. Forty-five minutes later, the waiter said that the oven was broken and still wasn't working. Why didn't he tell me that when I sat down?

P28 When in the military, my unit was traveling to New Jersey to fly to Germany. We went to a restaurant and sat in groups of eight. When the waitress came to our table, she was carrying a tray of water glasses. As she turned toward a beckoning coworker, she dumped the tray of eight glasses of water in my lap. I had to fly in a wet uniform.

P29 At a steakhouse, it was my grandmother's birthday. Most everyone had the food bar for dinner except for my sister and I, who ordered a dish. They never brought it to us. We eventually asked three times and then just decided to eat food off the food bar.

P30 We sat for 45 minutes before we were waited on, and then the waitress forgot she was waiting on our table. After another 30 minutes, we asked to see the manager.

Critical Incidents of Good Performance

G01   This waitress knew her stuff. I asked her what type of salad dressing they had, and off the top of her head she named all 12. I asked her what was on draft and she named all six beers.

G02   This waiter promptly brought us everything we asked for. We never really had to wait for anything.

G03   This waiter was full of life. While waiting on us he did some magic tricks!

G04   The waitress brought a new drink every time my drink was half-empty. I forgot to ask for my sandwich without lettuce and tomato. I was taking it off and she insisted on bringing me a whole new sandwich.

G05   The waitress regularly checked on us to see if we needed anything.

G06   The waiter joked with us and carried on polite conversation throughout our meal.

G07   She kept our beverages filled and checked back frequently without interrupting our dinner conversation.

G08   This waiter was very enthusiastic when we were first seated. After that, he was very kind and enthusiastic throughout the dinner.

G09   When we were out to dinner with a 3-year old boy, a server went out of her way to make the dinner nice. She brought the child several small toys and crayons to play with.

G10   The waitress checked with us every 10 minutes to make sure we had everything we needed. I never had to ask to fill my beer or wait to get my check.

G11   The waitress brought our food out in good sequence. When we finished our appetizers, she brought out the salad, and when we were finished with the salad she brought our meal.

G12   The waitress was very polite and courteous. She always had a smile. She seemed to actually care that our group enjoyed the time we spent at the restaurant.

G13   When we complained that it was taking too long for our food to arrive, the waiter gave us a free appetizer.

G14   The waiter kept our drinks full without us even having to ask for more.

G15   The waiter knew me because I had been to the restaurant so often. He would bring me what I wanted before I asked for it.

G16   The server was very friendly, courteous, and prompt. We had mentioned we planned on having dessert at the initial contact, and the server came by halfway through our meal and gave us a free dessert that had been prepared by mistake.

G17   The waiter made the evening special by giving added value to the event. He made an event out of serving me each course and had the staff sing happy birthday as he asked me to dance with him. He was entertaining and very attentive.

G18   This waiter was friendly and had a great sense of humor. He was always making jokes and kidding around.

G19   This waitress went out of her way to ask us what we needed and to get anything we wanted.

G20   The waitress was very professional. She was always available for me to ask for things but didn't keeping bothering me by asking how I was doing every 10 seconds.

G21   I ordered a steak well done and it came out really pink. I asked them to take it back and cook it a little more. The waiter brought the steak back out, made sure that it was cooked properly, and then took the price of the steak off our bill.

G22   The waitress came back time after time for drink refills and to see if everything was all right.

G23   It was my birthday, and the waiter made a big deal of singing me happy birthday and bringing me a small piece of birthday cake (for free).

G24   The waiter addressed me and my children in a respectful manner. He had a great conversation with my kids and treated them as if they were special.

G25   After the third time I visited this restaurant, the waitress asked me my name and then greeted me by name each time I returned to the restaurant. It made me feel like they really wanted my business.

G26   The restaurant was terribly busy. It took about 30 minutes to get our appetizer, so the waitress apologized and gave us each a complimentary drink.

G27   The waiter seemed to know everything about the menu. When I asked what was in a particular dish, he knew. He could even pronounce those weird Italian dishes!

G28   I was on a first date and was really getting into some great conversation with my date. The waitress seemed to sense this and was very good about being attentive yet not interrupting our conversation.

G29   The waiter was so funny. He would tell jokes, was always smiling, and had such a good enthusiastic attitude. The meal was great because of his personality — both my date and the food were mediocre.

G30   I am not a wine drinker, and the waiter knew a lot about the menu. He suggested a good wine to go with the meal I was ordering and could answer all of our questions about the contents of the dishes (I am allergic to tomatoes, so it is important that I know what is in each dish).

Exercise 2.5
Designing a Job Evaluation System

In your text, you learned that one of the first steps in designing a fair system of compensation is to determine the worth of a series of jobs. To do this with the point method, each job must be evaluated on a series of dimensions called *compensable factors*. As discussed in your text, the nature of these factors varies from system to system. It is the purpose of this exercise to provide you with a chance to think about the types of factors that make certain jobs worth more than others.

Either alone or with a group of your classmates, use the information in your text to design a compensation system that is based on the factors that you believe should determine the worth of a job. For this exercise:

a) Develop your list of compensable factors (e.g., responsibility, education). Most compensation systems contain between five and ten compensable factors.

	Compensable Factor
1	
2	
3	
4	
5	
6	
7	
8	
9	
10	
11	
12	

b) **Determine the degrees/levels for each factor.**

Factor   Degree/Level

1. _____   _____

_____

_____

_____

_____

_____

6. _____   _____
                            _____
                            _____
                            _____
                            _____

7. _____   _____
                            _____
                            _____
                            _____
                            _____

8. _____   _____
                            _____
                            _____
                            _____
                            _____

9. _____   _____
                            _____
                            _____
                            _____
                            _____

10. _____   _____
                           _____
                           _____
                           _____
                           _____

11. _____   _____
                           _____
                           _____
                           _____
                           _____

12. _____   _____
                           _____
                           _____

c)   Assign point values for each factor and for each degree within the factor. Write your point values next to each factor and degree on the previous pages.

Exercise 2.6
Determining Pay Equity

Once a point system has been developed and jobs have been evaluated, the next step in the job evaluation process is to ensure that employees in the jobs with the most number of points are being paid the highest salaries. As discussed in your text, this is usually done by charting the number of points a job is worth with the average current salary of the people in that job.

A wage trend line is then drawn that represents where each job should fall if it is paid fairly. Jobs falling well above the line are considered to be overpaid, and those falling well below the line are considered to be underpaid. The line is drawn by using a regression equation to use point values to predict salaries. For the purpose of this exercise, assume that you have performed a regression analysis on the data found on the following page. This analysis yielded the following formula:

$$\text{salary} = -8900 + (67.0 * \text{the number of points})$$

To draw your wage trend line, enter 400, 500, and 600 points into the equation to obtain their predicted salaries. For example, if you entered 450 points in the equation, the predicted salary would be:

$$\text{salary} = -8900 + (67.0 * 450) = -8900 + 30{,}150 = \$21{,}250$$

You would then plot the points and the predicted salary on the chart on the next page. Now, enter 400, 500, and 600 points into the above equation and place the predicted salaries below.

        400 points   _____ (predicted salary)

        500 points   _____ (predicted salary)

        600 points   _____ (predicted salary)

Plot these three data points on the graph on the next page, and then draw a line through the three points. This line is your wage trend line. When your line is drawn, plot the data found on the next page. Then use your graph to identify which jobs are currently being underpaid and which jobs are currently being overpaid.

Job	Points	Salary
Computer Operator	450	$18,000
Computer Programmer	550	$26,000
Tape Librarian	400	$16,000
Secretary I	500	$17,000
Secretary II	450	$15,000
Computer Analyst	600	$28,000
Clerk	350	$16,000
Supervisor	650	$32,000
Account Representative	500	$18,000
Customer Service Agent	550	$25,000

```
Salary
$35,000  -    -    -    -    -    -    -    -
$34,000  -    -    -    -    -    -    -    -
$33,000  -    -    -    -    -    -    -    -
$32,000  -    -    -    -    -    -    -    -
$31,000  -    -    -    -    -    -    -    -
$30,000  -    -    -    -    -    -    -    -
$29,000  -    -    -    -    -    -    -    -
$28,000  -    -    -    -    -    -    -    -
$27,000  -    -    -    -    -    -    -    -
$26,000  -    -    -    -    -    -    -    -
$25,000  -    -    -    -    -    -    -    -
$24,000  -    -    -    -    -    -    -    -
$23,000  -    -    -    -    -    -    -    -
$22,000  -    -    -    -    -    -    -    -
$21,000  -    -    -    -    -    -    -    -
$20,000  -    -    -    -    -    -    -    -
$19,000  -    -    -    -    -    -    -    -
$18,000  -    -    -    -    -    -    -    -
$17,000  -    -    -    -    -    -    -    -
$16,000  -    -    -    -    -    -    -    -
$15,000  -    -    -    -    -    -    -    -
$14,000  -    -    -    -    -    -    -    -
$13,000  -    -    -    -    -    -    -    -
$12,000  -    -    -    -    -    -    -    -
$11,000  -    -    -    -    -    -    -    -
$10,000  -    -    -    -    -    -    -    -
         300  350  400  450  500  550  600  650
                  Job Evaluation Points
```

Exercise 3.1
Federally Protected Classes

Your text indicated that several groups were protected by federal equal opportunity legislation. In these examples, indicate whether the group in question would be considered a *federally* protected class. In making your decision, do not take into account who you think would win the case. Instead, base your answer only on whether the person making the complaint is in a federally protected class. Assume that each organization has at least 15 employeees.

	Federally Protected Class?	
1. A World War II veteran claims he was discriminated against because he was in the war.	No	Yes
2. A Mormon says his religion forbids him to work on certain days.	No	Yes
3. A person who is hearing impaired claims she is disabled.	No	Yes
4. A gay applicant wasn't hired because of his sexual orientation.	No	Yes
5. A male wasn't hired for a sales position in a retail store specializing in women's shoes.	No	Yes
6. A 24-year old woman wasn't hired for a managerial position because she was too young.	No	Yes
7. A Norwegian applicant claimed he wasn't hired because a Chinese restaurant hired only Asians.	No	Yes
8. A light-skinned African American would not hire a dark-skinned African American.	No	Yes
9. A store wouldn't hire anyone with a college degree because it thought they were snobs.	No	Yes
10. A fast-food chain refused to hire any males with long hair.	No	Yes

Exercise 3.2
Determining Adverse Impact

For several years, Dexter's Knife Company required that all employees hired for quality control positions in their production facility in Miami have *at least* two years of college. The company's justification for this requirement is that because their cashiers must add prices in their head, they need to be educated. Even though they are the only production facility with this requirement, they are able to attract many applicants because they pay $3 an hour more than any other manufacturer.

In May of 2009, Valerie Castillo applied for a job with Dexter's and was not hired because she had never attended college. Ms. Castillo, a Hispanic woman, filed charges of discrimination with the EEOC. On the basis of the facts stated above, as well as the data below, will the EEOC investigation reveal adverse impact on the basis of either sex or race? Assume that any applicant with two or more years of college was hired.

Applicant	Sex	Ethnicity	Years of College
Mike Donovan	Male	White	0
Jamie Jaworski	Female	White	0
Matt Chambers	Male	White	0
Jorge Castillo	Male	Hispanic	0
Valerie Castillo	Female	Hispanic	0
Santos Jiminez	Male	Hispanic	0
Jose Garza	Male	Hispanic	0
Juan Rinez	Male	Hispanic	1
Alex Timmons	Male	White	1
Gene Marshall	Male	White	1
Cindy Landon	Female	White	1
Emmett Meridian	Male	White	2
Brian Moser	Male	White	2
Roger Hicks	Male	White	2
Robert Thacher	Male	White	2
Marcus White	Male	White	2
Oscar Sota	Male	Hispanic	2
Joseph Sapeda	Male	White	2
Ken Olsen	Male	White	2
Esteban Famosa	Male	Hispanic	3
Teo Famosa	Male	Hispanic	3
Lila West	Female	White	3
Oscar Prado	Male	White	3
Fred "Freebo" Bowman	Male	White	3
Nathan Martin	Male	White	3
Little Chino	Male	Hispanic	4
Ethan Turner	Male	White	4
Clemson Galt	Male	White	4
Camilla Figg	Female	White	4
Miguel Prado	Male	Hispanic	4

Exercise 3.3
Responses to Adverse Impact

In the text you learned that, if adverse impact occurs, an employment practice can still be legal if it is job related (valid), is the result of a *bona fide* seniority system, is in use due to national security concerns, or was implemented to provide veterans with preferential hiring. In these examples, indicate the extent to which you think the employment practice will be found to be legal.

A. Applicants for patrol officer positions with the city of Fort Worth, Texas, are administered a cognitive ability test. The average score on the test is 70. All applicants who served in the U.S. armed forces automatically get 10 points added to their scores. Adverse impact occurs because 20% of male applicants and 5% of female applicants are veterans. Is this practice legal? Why or why not?

_____

_____

_____

_____

B. The cognitive ability test described above also results in adverse impact because 80% of White applicants pass the test compared to 60% of African American applicants. Scores on the test correlate significantly ($r = .45$) with performance in the police academy. None of the other tests looked at by the City predicted academy or job performance. Is this practice legal? Why or why not?

_____

_____

_____

_____

C. According to the contract between the union and the company, every employment decision at the Spears School of Driving is based on seniority. That is, the employees who have been at Spears the longest get first opportunity for promotions, working the day shift, and not working overtime. Due to a decline in business, Spears must lay off 20 employees. On the basis of seniority, 10 of these employees are African American and 10 are White. Of the 200 employees who will keep their jobs, 180 are White and 20 are African American. Is this practice legal? Why or why not?

_____

_____

_____

_____

Exercise 3.4
Legality of Employment Practices

Use the legal issues flowchart in Figure 3.2 on page 81 of your text to decide if the following situations would be legal. Be sure to state your logic at *each stage* of the flowchart.

1. Chef Gordon Ramsey is boiling mad at his HR manager. The manager will not hire anyone whose shoes are not well polished when they come to the interview. Ramsey doesn't know how the manager cooked up such a requirement and has been stewing about whether the requirement is legal. What would you tell him?

2. A court system is about to fill an opening for the position of Victim's Advocate. The position involves working with women who have been sexually assaulted. The court has decided that it will only fill the position with a female because all of the victims are women and the crimes were sexual in nature. Would this be legal?

3. To get a job at the Arsonville Fire Department, applicants must pass a mechanical ability test. An extensive study found that the test correlates significantly (r = .30) with performance. During the current testing period, 20% of male applicants and 10% of female applicants passed the test. The Fire Department tried to find a test with less adverse impact but was unable to do so. Would the use of the test be legal?

Exercise 3.5
Sexual Harassment

In Chapter 3, you learned that there are two types of sexual harassment, quid pro quo and hostile environment. In the situations below, indicate if the situation represents a case of quid pro quo, hostile environment, or no sexual harassment.

A. A supervisor tells his assistant that if she won't sleep with him, she will never get a raise or a promotion.

   Quid pro quo   Hostile environment   No sexual harassment

   _____
   _____
   _____

B. At least twice a week during work hours, Fred tells Britney that she looks nice. Britney is a bit of a flirt and seems to like the attention Fred gives her.

   Quid pro quo   Hostile environment   No sexual harassment

   _____
   _____
   _____

C. Judy asks Brian out on a date. He is not really interested in her and he declines. For the next two months, Judy asks Brian out every week and each time he says no. He is so tired of the situation that he brings the matter to his supervisor.

   Quid pro quo   Hostile environment   No sexual harassment

   _____
   _____
   _____

D. John usually addresses his female coworkers as "honey."

   Quid pro quo   Hostile environment   No sexual harassment

   _____
   _____
   _____

Exercise 3.6
Understanding Affirmative Action

The personnel director at East High School thinks she is in big trouble. Ten years ago, 30% of the residents in the county were Hispanic yet only 5% of school employees were Hispanic. To remedy this situation, the school system developed an affirmative action program in which at least 40% of all new hires were to be Hispanic. The program had been working well because today 25% of all school employees are Hispanic compared to 28% in the qualified work force.

Last week, however, a white employee who wasn't hired for a teaching job filed a lawsuit challenging the legality of the affirmative action plan. Troy Bolton claimed that he was more qualified than the minority applicant who received the job. Bolton had a 3.4 college GPA and three years of teaching experience whereas George Lopez, the minority applicant, had only a 3.2 GPA and two years of experience. Should our personnel director be worried? Why or why not? Use the flowchart on page 102 of your text (Figure 3.4) as a guide. Be sure to discuss your decision at each step of the flowchart.

Exercise 3.7
Employee Privacy Issues

In Chapter 3, you learned that drug testing, office and locker searches, psychological testing, and electronic surveillance can pose potential legal problems due to invasion of privacy. In the following examples, indicate whether you think an invasion of privacy occurred.

A. A retail store places cameras in each corner of the store to prevent shoplifting and employee theft. The only place the cameras can't see are the dressing rooms. Is this an invasion of privacy? Why or why not?

_____
_____
_____

B. During a polygraph test, a police department asks applicants how many people they slept with in the past five years. Is this an invasion of privacy? Why or why not?

_____
_____
_____

C. A manufacturing company assigns each employee a locker and requires that the employees provide their own combination locks. The company suspects that several of the employees are drinking on the job, so it cuts the locks and inspects the lockers. Is this an invasion of privacy? Why or why not?

_____
_____
_____

D. Siesta County has a new drug testing policy in which, weekly, it will require 30 randomly chosen employees to provide a urine sample. To ensure that the employees are not cheating, a monitor will observe the employee as he or she provides the urine specimen. Is this an invasion of privacy? Why or why not?

_____
_____
_____

Exercise 3.8
Testing Your Legal Knowledge

You have just been hired as the employment law expert for a new NBC call-in show, *Can I Sue?* What would you tell the caller asking the following questions? Be sure to include the rationale for your answer as well as the law on which you are basing your answer.

1. I am one of 25 employees in my company. I want to have a baby but my boss says that the company will not grant me leave. Can they do this?

2. I was burned badly as a child, and as a result, I have scars all over my face. I can't seem to get a job at McDonald's, Wendy's, or Burger King because they think my looks will turn off the customers. Can they do that to me?

3. My male supervisor walks behind all of his employees and rubs their shoulders before asking, "How is it going today?" Isn't this sexual harassment?

4. A woman at work has sent me 15 love letters. After the third letter, I told her to stop. She continued sending the letters that included such statements as "I have enjoyed watching you so much over these past few months" and "I constantly imagine us in bed together." Isn't this sexual harassment?

5. Nine months ago I was refused a job. I think it was because I am Italian. Can I file a complaint with the EEOC?

Exercise 4.1
Reading Help-Wanted Ads

Your text discussed the types of help-wanted advertisements that can be found in a newspaper. From a recent copy of your local newspaper, find examples of each type of ad and tape them to the spaces below.

Send-resume   Respond-by-calling

Apply-in-person   Blind-box

Exercise 4.2
Writing Help-Wanted Advertisements

The recruitment manager for "Pay 'n Pray," a new fast-food chain, has asked you to develop a help-wanted advertisement that will increase the number of applicants who apply for customer service positions with the restaurant. In the space below, design your help-wanted advertisement.

Exercise 4.3
Point of Purchase Recruitment

Your text discussed the popularity of point of purchase recruitment techniques. As you go to the mall, drive down the road, or eat at restaurants, note the examples of point of purchase recruiting that you see. If possible, attach copies of the techniques (such as tray liners) that you encounter. Do not remove things (such as table tents) that are not designed to be taken.

Location	Point of Purchase Technique

What did you notice about the techniques? What types of applicants did they try to attract?

Exercise 4.4
Employee Recruitment

Your text discussed a number of methods that organizations use to recruit employees. The purpose of this exercise is to provide you with an opportunity to develop a recruitment program.

The Situation

The McBurger King restaurant chain has serious personnel problems. Each franchise is designed to employ 30 employees as cooks and counter helpers. Unfortunately, all of the franchises are having difficulty recruiting employees because they can pay only minimum wage.

As Assistant Personnel Director, you have been asked to develop a novel recruitment strategy to solve this problem. In addition to using the methods discussed in your text, try to design a recruitment strategy that is both practical and creative. Discuss your strategy and provide examples of your ads and your innovative creations.

Exercise 4.5
Identifying KSAOs

In Chapter 2 of your text, there is a sample job description in Table 2.1 Use this job description, one that you wrote for the Chapter 2 exercise, or one for your current job to begin to create a structured interview. List the essential KSAOs for the job, and then indicate which of the KSAOs would best be tapped in an interview.

KSAO	Best tapped in an interview?
_____	yes no
_____	yes no
_____	yes no
_____	yes no
_____	yes no
_____	yes no
_____	yes no
_____	yes no
_____	yes no
_____	yes no
_____	yes no
_____	yes no

Exercise 4.6
Developing Interview Questions

After completing Exercise 4.5, you have identified the essential KSAOs for the job and determined which of the KSAOs are best tapped in an interview. To get you started, for each of the examples below, indicate the *type* of structured interview question that it represents. You can use Figure 4.9 in your text as a guide.

a. _____ I see on your resume that you belonged to the Ryder Club. What is the Ryder Club?

b. _____ How would you rename an Excel file?

c. _____ Tell me about a time when you had to manage multiple tasks.

d. _____ Suppose a customer told you that he wanted a refund on his meal because it wasn't cooked properly. What would you do?

e. _____ Imagine that you are a teller and the line of customers is getting too long for you to handle before your lunch break. What would you do?

f. _____ What are the components needed to install a telephone?

g. _____ On your resume your job at Sears ended in June 1998 and your next job at Belk started in October 1998. What were you doing between June and October?

h. _____ The job of research assistant involves a lot of stress. Tell me how you have handled stressful jobs in the past.

i. _____ Can you work every other weekend?

j. _____ What is the ideal work environment for you?

Now that you can identify different types of questions, the next step is to actually write questions that will tap each KSAO identified in the previous exercise. In the space below, write two examples of each type of interview question.

Disqualifier

1. _____
   _____
   _____
   _____

2. _____
   _____
   _____
   _____

Skill level determiner

1. _____
   _____
   _____
   _____

2. _____
   _____
   _____
   _____

Future focused (situational)

1. _____

2. _____

Past focused (behavioral)

1. _____

2. _____

Organizational fit

1. _____
   _____
   _____
   _____
   _____

2. _____
   _____
   _____
   _____
   _____

Clarifiers

Use the resume on the following page to write your clarifiers. You will probably have more than two of these to ask.

1. _____
   _____

2. _____
   _____

3. _____
   _____

4. _____
   _____

Matthew "Bucky" Crenshaw
27122 East Bay Ridge Road
Radford, VA 24141
(540) 555-5656

Professional Strengths
- Five years of customer service experience
- Good math skills
- Get along well with people
- Supervisory experience
- Can work any kind of cash register

Work Experience
Sales Associate (January 2009 – present)
J.C. Penney, Christiansburg, VA
   Responsibilities include helping customers with their purchases, stocking   shelves, and taking inventory.

Salesperson (March 2007 – May 2008)
Ties for Guys, Roanoke, VA
   Helped customers find ties that best matched their shirts and suits. Received three raises.

Teller (August 2004 – February 2007)
Pulaski Community Bank, Pulaski, VA
   Responsible for opening new accounts, helping customers with transactions, and ensuring that the teller drawer is accurate. Left to take better paying job.

Education
High School Diploma (2004)
John Wayne High School, Tustin, CA

Exercise 4.7
Scoring Interview Questions

After writing your interview questions in Exercise 4.6, the next step is to develop the key for scoring answers to the questions. To provide you with practice in developing a scoring key, choose two of your questions and use a typical answers approach to score one and a key issues approach to score the other.

Typical Answers Approach

5 _____
 _____
 _____

4 _____
 _____
 _____

3 _____
 _____
 _____

2 _____
 _____
 _____

1 _____
 _____
 _____

Key Issues Approach

Exercise 4.8
Finding Career Resources

Because job hunting can be difficult, most universities have a Career Services Center to help students write resumes, practice interviews, and find potential jobs. Stop by the Career Services Center at your university and find the following information.

What is the name of the person in charge?	
What hours are they open?	
What is their web address?	
What services do they offer?	
Do they have on-line resume services? Which ones?	
What resources do they have for people in your field?	
When are the upcoming job fairs scheduled?	
For which majors are these job fairs best suited?	
What organizations will be at the job fairs that might be of interest to you?	
Signature of person you spoke with	

Exercise 4.9
Surviving the Employment Interview

These next few exercises are designed to help improve your chances of performing well in your future employment interviews.

A. **Learning About the Organization** Think of a large company for which you would like to work upon graduation. Now go to the library and to your Career Services Center on campus and get some information about the company. Once you have done this, write down the highlights of what you have learned below. What you write down and remember will be used later during the interview.	
Name of the organization:	
Information you learned:	
Sources of information you used:	
B. **Dressing for the Interview**	
If you were to interview tomorrow and did not have a chance to purchase new clothes, what would you wear to the interview?	
If you were to interview in a month, what would be your ideal "interview uniform"?	
C. **Answering Commonly Asked Questions** Below you will find a series of questions that are often asked during the employment interview. Next to each question, indicate how you would respond if asked the question during an actual interview.	
1. Why are you interested in working for our company?	
2. What do you know about us?	
3. Why did you choose your major?	
4. What do you consider to be your greatest strengths?	
5. What do you consider to be your greatest weakness?	
6. Where do you want to be 5 years from now?	
7. What subjects did you like best in school?	
8. How would you describe your leadership style?	
9. If you could change anything about your current job, what would it be?	
10. What do you like most about your current job?	
D. **Asking Questions of the Interviewer** At the end of the interview, the interviewer usually asks if the interviewee has any questions. In the space below, write eight questions that you might ask the interviewer.	
1.	
2.	
3.	
4.	
5.	
6.	
7.	
8.	

Exercise 4.10
Resume Writing

Your text discussed an excellent format to use in writing your resume. Keeping the text example in mind, use the sheets on the next few pages to outline your resume. Once you have outlined your resume, type it on a separate piece of paper. If you are having difficulty thinking of things to list, it is a sign that you need to get involved in more activities and/or get some relevant work experience.

Professional Strengths

The first section in your resume is the professional strengths section. If you remember from the text, this section is designed to be a summary of your strengths and relevant experiences. This summary is based on the psychological principles of primacy (establishing a good first impression), priming (preparing the reader to expect good things), impression formation, and memory organization.

The following are examples of strengths often listed by students:

- Bachelor's degree in psychology
- Leadership experience
- Two years supervisory experience
- Computer literate (BASIC, WordPerfect, Lotus)
- Conversational in Spanish
- Six years work experience
- Active in the community
- Excellent oral and written communication skills
- Counseling experience

Write your professional strengths below.

-
-
-
-
-
-

Education

The next section of your resume is a summary of your education. This section first involves listing your degree, your major, your graduation date (or anticipated date), and the university from which you will graduate. The next part of the section contains your educational highlights. These highlights might include your GPA, minor, papers written, activities, and clubs. Limit this list to no more than seven items (again, we are taking accommodating the limits of short-term memory). The beauty of this section is that you can include highlights from high school, junior college, and college. An example of this section would be:

B.A., Psychology (May, 2003)
Pepperdine University, Malibu, California

Highlights:
- 3.22 GPA
- Minor in business
- Wrote research paper on mental retardation
- President, high school student government

- Secretary of Psychology Club
     - Chair of three fraternity committees
     - Worked to help finance education

Complete the section below for yourself.

B.S., Name of your university (date)
Location of your university
Highlights:
•
•
•
•
•
•

Professional Experience

The final section of your resume contains information on your professional experience and/or your work experience. Of course, it would be great if all of your experience was related to your career, but this is seldom the case. Instead, most college students have had part-time and summer jobs at places such as McDonald's and Sears. However, if you have done career-related volunteer work, it can be placed in this section. An example of a job listing would be:

    <u>Youth Counselor</u> (Summer, 2008)
    Star-Bright Summer Camp, Hog Eye, Arkansas
        Major responsibilities for this summer camp designed to improve reading
    levels of mentally retarded teens centered on the supervision and teaching of 12
    developmentally challenged teens. Specific duties included helping campers
    get dressed, leading games and sports, teaching reading skills, counseling youths about
    problems such as homesickness, and completing daily status reports.
        Accomplishments included having only one camper not improve his reading
    level and being awarded a plaque as "Counselor of the Year."

Complete this last section for your own jobs.

Exercise 4.11
Classroom Exercise: Scoring a Structured Interview

Your instructor will show a video of two applicants for a restaurant server position going through a structured interview. Use the scoring key below to score how well the interviewees perform. Compare your scores with those of your classmates. How consistent were you? How could this interview be improved?

Question	Sarah King	Amy Dobkins
1		
2		
3		
4		
5		
6		
7		
Total Points		

Comments and Suggestions for Improvement

Sarah King

Q1: Tell me about your previous restaurant experience.
5	Has more than 1 year of experience as a server in a high-class restaurant
4	Has less than 1 year of experience as a server in a high-class restaurant
3	Has more than 1 year of experience in a restaurant that was not a high-class restaurant
2	Has less than one year of experience in a restaurant that was not a high class restaurant
1	Has no experience as a server in a restaurant

Q2: At your previous serving jobs, about what percent of the bill did you receive in tips?
5	Over 19%
4	16-19%
3	15%
3	Tips were distributed among employees
2	Less than 15%
1	Never received tips at a previous job

Q3: What hours are you available to work?
5	Any shift and any day
4	Nights and weekends only
3	Nights or weekends ony
2	Days only
1	Never on Saturday or Sunday

Q4: Suppose that a customer received a steak that was not cooked properly, what would you do?
5	Apologize, offer to get the customer a new steak, and remove the steak from the bill if the customer seems upset
4	Apologize, offer to get the customer a new steak, and automatically remove the steak from the bill
3	Apologize and offer to get the customer a new steak
2	Get the customer a new steak
1	Apologize to the customer

Q5: Suppose that you have a very angry customer, what would you do? (Give a point for each strategy that the applicant mentions and a point if the applicant gives all the answers in the proper order)
1	Let the customer vent, listen
1	Apologize for the problem
1	Ask the customer what you can do to solve the problem
1	Do what the customer asks (within reason)
1	Answers were given in the proper order

Q6: You notice that a customer's glass of iced tea is half-empty. What should you do?
5	Ask if the customer would like some more tea (applicant also provides the reason that one should ask)
4	Ask if the customer would like some more tea
3	Bring a new glass of tea
2	Fill the customer's glass
1	Wait until the glass is empty

Q7: Restaurant Knowledge: Give one point for each correct answer		
	What type of wine (red, white) goes best with a marinara sauce?	Red
	What is in a White Russian?	Vodka, Kahlua, cream
	On which side of the plate does the salad fork go?	Left side
	An Italian dish with the word *pollo* contains what?	chicken
	A customer asks for a white wine; would you give him the Chardonnay or the Merlot?	Chardonnay
	Should the tip be computed before or after taxes have been added?	Before
	What should a steak cooked medium look like?	A little pink inside
	What is calamari?	Squid
	Can a parent order a glass of wine for her underage child?	No
	Which of these spices would not be considered sweet: basil, tarragon, fennel, or cloves?	Cloves

Amy Dobkins

Q1: Tell me about your previous restaurant experience.
	5	Has more than 1 year of experience as a server in a high-class restaurant
	4	Has less than 1 year of experience as a server in a high-class restaurant
	3	Has more than 1 year of experience in a restaurant that was not a high-class restaurant
	2	Has less than one year of experience in a restaurant that was not a high class restaurant
	1	Has no experience as a server in a restaurant

Q2: At your previous serving jobs, about what percent of the bill did you receive in tips?
	5	Over 19%
	4	16-19%
	3	15%
	2	Less than 15%
	1	Never received tips at a previous job

Q3: What hours are you available to work?
	5	Any shift and any day
	4	Nights and weekends only
	3	Nights or weekends
	2	Days only
	1	Never on Saturday or Sunday

Q4: Suppose that a customer received a steak that was not cooked properly, what would you do?
	5	Apologize, offer to get the customer a new steak, and remove the steak from the bill if the customer seems upset
	4	Apologize, offer to get the customer a new steak, and automatically remove the steak from the bill
	3	Apologize and offer to get the customer a new steak
	2	Get the customer a new steak
	1	Apologize to the customer

Q5: Suppose that you have a very angry customer, what would you do? (Give a point for each strategy that the applicant mentions and a point if the applicant gives all the answers in the proper order)
	1	Let the customer vent, listen
	1	Apologize for the problem
	1	Ask the customer what you can do to solve the problem
	1	Do what the customer asks (within reason)
	1	Answers were given in the proper order

Q6: You notice that a customer's glass of iced tea is half-empty. What should you do?
	5	Ask if the customer would like some more tea (applicant also provides the reason that one should ask)
	4	Ask if the customer would like some more tea
	3	Bring a new glass of tea
	2	Fill the customer's glass
	1	Wait until the glass is empty

Q7: Restaurant Knowledge: Give one point for each correct answer		
	What type of wine (red, white) goes best with a marinara sauce?	*Red*
	What is in a White Russian?	*Vodka, Kahlua, cream*
	On which side of the plate does the salad fork go?	*Left side*
	An Italian dish with the word *pollo* contains what?	*chicken*
	A customer asks for a white wine; would you give him the Chardonnay or the Merlot?	*Chardonnay*
	Should the tip be computed before or after taxes have been added?	*Before*
	What should a steak cooked medium look like?	*A little pink inside*
	What is calamari?	*Squid*
	Can a parent order a glass of wine for her underage child?	*No*
	Which of these spices would not be considered sweet: basil, tarragon, fennel, or cloves?	*Cloves*

Exercise 5.1
Trait Approach

In Chapter 6, the trait approach to scoring letters of recommendation was discussed. Below, you will find two letters of recommendation. Score each of the letters using the trait approach by underlining the traits and then counting the number of traits in each of the five categories. Which of the applicants would you hire for the job of an accountant?

Dimension	Elijah Craig	James Beam
Mental Agility	____	____
Vigor	____	____
Urbanity	____	____
Cooperation-Consideration	____	____
Dependability-Reliability	____	____

Dear Mr. Daniels:

It is a pleasure to write this letter in support of Mr. Elijah Craig. I have known Elijah for 10 years as he was an accounting associate in our firm.

Elijah is a very dependable, careful, and precise person. He amazes all of us at the office with his attention to detail and with the accuracy of his reports. To the best of my knowledge, Elijah always has his work completed on time. Elijah is a considerate employee who is a real team player.

If you have any questions or need more information about Elijah, please let me know.

Dear Mr. Daniels:

It is a pleasure to write this letter in support of Mr. James Beam. I have known Jim for 10 years as he was an accounting associate in our firm.

Jim is one of the most intelligent, original, and creative individuals I have ever met. He is always developing new ideas. In addition to being so smart, Jim has a great sense of humor, is very friendly, and always cheerful.

If you have any questions or need more information about Jim, please let me know.

Exercise 5.2
Cognitive Ability

One of the best predictors of performance is cognitive ability. The following few pages contain sample items from the Basic Cognitive Ability Test (BCAT). The BCAT is used by career advisers to test employees' basic skills.

Section I: Basic Math

Circle the correct answer for each of the math questions. You may NOT use a calculator.

1. A bus is traveling 60 miles per hour. How many miles down the road will the bus be in 5 minutes?
    a) 5 miles   b) 6 miles   c) 12 miles   d) none of the above

2. It takes 25 minutes to cut and style someone's hair. If you cut and styled nine customers' hair in 1day, how many minutes would you have spent working?
    a) 125   b) 175   c) 225   d) none of the above

3. A pharmaceutical company sells a drug to a store for $9.00 per dose. The store increases the price it charges customers to $20 per dose. How much profit would the store make on the 20 doses?
    a) $40   b) $400   c) $580   d) none of the above

4. If it costs 16 cents a minute to call from 5 p.m. to 11 p.m. and 10 cents per minute to call from 11:00 p.m. to 8:00 a.m., how much would it cost if a person talked to a friend from 10:52 p.m. to 11:18 p.m.?
    a) $2.98   b) $3.00   c) $3.08   d) none of the above

5. A customer gives you a Kennedy half-dollar, a five dollar bill, three dimes, six nickels, and four pennies. How much did the customer give you?
    a) $6.04   b) $6.10   c) $6.14   d) none of the above

Section IV: Logic

6. What number would come next?
    46   42   38   34   _____

7. Which of the following words does not fit with the others?   _____
    creek   stream   river   lake   brook

    James King is 5'9" tall. Kelly King is 5'7" tall. Kelly's brother, Steven, is 2 inches taller than James. James' uncle, Dave, is the same height as Kelly. Dave's wife, Patty, is the same height as Steven.

8. Kelly is James' wife.
    a) True   b) False   c) not enough information

9. Dave is taller than Kelly.
    a) True   b) False   c) not enough information

10. Dave is taller than his wife.
    a) True   b) False   c) not enough information

Section III: Vocabulary

For each of the following sentences, indicate which of the three words is most similar in meaning to the word that is bold faced.

11. Airline fares are constantly **fluctuating**.
    a) changing   b) increasing   c) decreasing

12. Hotels are now offering special **amenities**.
    a) prices   b) courtesies   c) schedules

13. Bob and Jane are my **colleagues**.
    a) neighbors   b) associates   c) friends

14. The **impasse** will not be easily settled.
    a) deadlock   b) argument   c) contest

15. He thought of himself as **omniscient**.
    a) all knowing   b) a scholar   c) versatile

Section IV: Grammar

For each of the sentences below, mark the letter of the part of the sentence that contains an error such as a misspelling, a grammatical error, or wrong punctuation. If there are no errors in the sentence, mark the letter "e" for correct.

16. They / were / the boys / books.   correct
    (a)   (b)   (c)   (d)   (e)

17. The car / was / moving / to fast.   correct
    (a)   (b)   (c)   (d)   (e)

18. We / believe she / is their / teacher.   correct
    (a) (b)   (c)   (d)   (e)

19. He would'nt / stop talking / about the / accident.   correct
    (a)   (b)   (c)   (d)   (e)

20. Your going / to be late / for the / meeting.   correct
    (a)   (b)   (c)   (d)   (e)

Exercise 5.3
Leaderless Group Discussion

As discussed in your text, assessment centers are often a useful method for predicting employee success on the job. One of the most common exercises in an assessment center is the leaderless group discussion. With a leaderless group discussion, several applicants are given a problem to discuss. As the group is discussing the problem, a group of assessors listens to the conversation and rates the quality of participation by each applicant.

Instructions

Below you will find a problem to use in a leaderless group discussion. Your professor will assign six students to take part in the discussion while the other students use the rating form on the following pages to evaluate the participation of each group member. Each observer should rate the behavior of two group members. Rather than use students in your class, your instructor might have you watch a video of a leaderless group discussion and rate two of the participants in the video.

Class Discussion Problem

IBM has noticed that their younger employees seem not to be as dedicated to their jobs as are older employees. The young employees tend to miss more work and often refuse to work overtime. Do you think this observation is valid, and if so, what can be done to change the attitudes and behavior of the younger workers?

Rating for Leaderless Group Discussion

Name of Group Member_____

Check all of the behaviors you observed for the person you were designated to watch.

Oral Communication
____ Made clear and concise comments (did not ramble)
____ Maintained eye contact
____ Voice easy to understand
____ Used proper grammar and vocabulary
____ Fully expressed thoughts
____ Was enthusiastic

Direction
____ Got the group started on the task
____ Ensured that the group was making progress
____ Made suggestions

Logic
____ Presented sound arguments
____ Pulled together related ideas

Sensitivity
____ Reinforced positive comments made by group members
____ Encouraged others to talk

Total number of positive behaviors checked _____

Comments

_____
_____
_____
_____

Rating for Leaderless Group Discussion

Name of Group Member _____

Check all of the behaviors you observed for the person you were designated to watch.

Oral Communication
____ Made clear and concise comments (did not ramble)
____ Maintained eye contact
____ Voice easy to understand
____ Used proper grammar and vocabulary
____ Fully expressed thoughts
____ Was enthusiastic

Direction
____ Got the group started on the task
____ Ensured that the group was making progress
____ Made suggestions

Logic
____ Presented sound arguments
____ Pulled together related ideas

Sensitivity
____ Reinforced positive comments made by group members
____ Encouraged others to talk

Total number of positive behaviors checked _____

Comments

_____
_____
_____
_____

Exercise 5.4
Personality Inventories

One of the techniques that can be used to select employees is personality tests. These types of tests are especially useful in jobs such as sales and teaching that involve interacting with people.

On the next page you will find the Employee Personality Inventory (EPI), a short personality test that is used mostly for seminars about understanding people but has also been fairly successful in predicting performance in several jobs.

Employee Personality Inventory

Choose the word in each pair that is most like you. Even if both words are like you, you must choose only one word. If neither word is like you, you must still choose one of the words. After completing the test, your instructor will show you how to score the test and then you can read about your personality type on the following few pages. Please note that the EPI may not be reproduced in any format without the written permission of the author of this text.

Thinking   _____

Directing   _____

Communicating   _____

Soothing   _____

Organizing   _____

1. ( ) Calm   ( ) Efficient
2. ( ) Accurate   ( ) Energetic
3. ( ) Original   ( ) Competitive
4. ( ) Introverted   ( ) Extroverted
5. ( ) Careful   ( ) Bold
6. ( ) Resourceful   ( ) Trusting
7. ( ) Empathic   ( ) Inquiring
8. ( ) Assertive   ( ) Exact
9. ( ) Playful   ( ) Dominant
10. ( ) Curious   ( ) Detailed
11. ( ) Precise   ( ) Tolerant
12. ( ) Ambitious   ( ) Helpful
13. ( ) Outgoing   ( ) Imaginative
14. ( ) Talkative   ( ) Agreeable
15. ( ) Enterprising   ( ) Friendly
16. ( ) Persuasive   ( ) Sociable
17. ( ) Patient   ( ) Convincing
18. ( ) Organized   ( ) Inventive
19. ( ) Conversational   ( ) Self-disciplined
20. ( ) Confident   ( ) Creative
21. ( ) Loyal   ( ) Chatty
22. ( ) Outspoken   ( ) Soft-spoken
23. ( ) Clever   ( ) Socializer
24. ( ) Powerful   ( ) Insightful
25. ( ) Dependable   ( ) Self-assured
26. ( ) Frisky   ( ) Intense
27. ( ) Peaceful   ( ) Smart
28. ( ) Spontaneous   ( ) Cautious
29. ( ) Innovative   ( ) Systematic
30. ( ) Orderly   ( ) Cooperative
31. ( ) Daring   ( ) Sincere
32. ( ) Methodical   ( ) Outgoing
33. ( ) Sharp   ( ) Fun
34. ( ) Rebellious   ( ) Punctual
35. ( ) Fun-loving   ( ) Fearless
36. ( ) Bright   ( ) Dynamic
37. ( ) Modest   ( ) Perceptive
38. ( ) Detailed   ( ) Ingenious
39. ( ) Mingler   ( ) Courteous
40. ( ) Supportive   ( ) Logical

© 1998 by Michael G. Aamodt, Ph.D. Reproduction in any form prohibited without written permission of the author

Thinkers

General Personality

Often called "rebels" or "mavericks" by others, Thinkers are creative, unconventional, insightful, inventive individuals who love the process of thinking, analyzing, and creating. They challenge the status quo, create new products and ideas, and provide new ways to think of things. Though they create new products and ideas, Thinkers consider the idea the end result and seldom get excited about the process of carrying through on a project. Thinkers hate schedules, dislike rules and policy, and have little need for authority. They are free spirits and independent thinkers who value freedom and require the latitude to do things "their way." Thinkers can often be identified by the notion that they always seem to be preoccupied with thought. They can walk right by a person without even seeing him.

Thinkers are interesting people in that of the five personality types they are the most difficult to predict. They are complex people who are not easily understood or categorized. However, they do make excellent artists, writers, computer programmers, troubleshooters, engineers, and marketing analysts.

Communication Style

Thinkers communicate with others by discussing ideas, being sarcastic, creating puns, and dreaming. Their communication style is a combination of the other four styles in that they tend to be friendly like the Communicator, adventurous like the Director, and introverted like the Soother. The best way to communicate with a Thinker is to discuss the "big picture." Do not get caught up in detail. Rather than being provided with solutions to problems up front, Thinkers should be asked what they think a good solution might be.

Leadership Style

Thinkers do not seek leadership positions but can become leaders because they are often the people with the best ideas. When they do become leaders, they lead through motivation and inspiration. Others get carried away by their ideas.

Strengths
- Ability to develop new ideas and systems
- Are not afraid of change
- Can see the "big picture"
- Are good problem solvers

Weaknesses Associated With Very High Scores or Stressful Situations
- May not carry through on their ideas
- Often have problems with rules and structure
- May not always be realistic
- Are easily bored and distracted

Directors

General Personality

Directors are fast-paced, efficient, confident, assertive individuals who are more interested in quantity than quality. Directors set high goals for themselves and for others. They are highly competitive: Doing well is not enough for Directors; they want to do better than everyone else. Directors are fearless and are willing to take chances—"play it safe" is a phrase seldom uttered by a Director. They tend to be independent and are much happier working alone than with others. Their greatest strength to an organization is that, when given a job to do, they will always get the job done ahead of schedule.

More than anything, Directors fear being taken advantage of and thus are not very trusting of others. Directors also tend to be impatient and easily agitated. As a result of this impatience and lack of trust, Directors are often considered to have poor interpersonal skills.

Communication Style

Directors communicate with others in a very direct fashion. They tend to dislike small talk, would prefer to "get right to the point," and prefer executive summaries rather than pages of detail. Directors communicate best if they are told the purpose of the meeting before it occurs. Directors use eye contact when they speak and like to be given more than an average amount of personal communication space. Directors are not good at picking up subtle hints or nonverbal cues so the best way to communicate with them is to look them in the eye and tell them exactly what you want. Directors should never be told they "must" do something as their automatic reaction is to resist threats to their freedom.

Leadership Style

Directors enjoy being "in charge" but are not always good at leadership. They tend to use a very directive style of leadership and rarely ask for the advice or approval of others. They set goals, provide direction, and expect a high level of performance from everyone. As leaders, Directors are good at quickly making tough decisions, exuding a "can do" attitude, and cutting through red tape.

Strengths

- Ability to get things done
- Willingness to take charge
- Ability to quickly make tough decisions
- Efficient use of time resulting in a high volume of work

Weaknesses Associated With Very High Scores or Stressful Situations
- Often are perceived as being too competitive
- Can be abrasive, impatient, and short with people
- Are often not good followers or team players
- Have a tendency to break rules and regulations

Communicators

General Personality

Communicators are outgoing, friendly, talkative individuals who are much more interested in people than they are in projects or paperwork. They get along well with other people and tend to mingle well in social situations. Because Communicators like fun and excitement, they are easily bored. As a result of their people skills, Communicators make excellent supervisors, teachers, and customer service representatives.

More than anything, Communicators fear not being liked and thus are not as direct with others as they at times need to be. Communicators need a lot of attention and often dislike sharing the limelight. Because of their preference for people as opposed to things, Communicators often delay work that involves data or reports.

Communication Style

Communicators talk with others in a very friendly, animated fashion. They tend to dislike business or serious discussions and would prefer to talk about fun things, exchange stories, and tell jokes. Thus, the best way to talk to a communicator is to start the conversation with an interesting topic and then slowly move toward the actual topic. Communicators are very expressive when they speak.

Leadership Style

Communicators do not necessarily seek leadership positions but often find themselves being chosen as a leader because they are well liked by others. When placed in charge, Communicators will usually adopt a participative leadership style in which they will probably call a meeting and ask for feedback from the people involved with the problem or decision.

Strengths

- Ability to talk with anyone about anything (good mingling skills)
- Good sense of humor
- Are well liked
- Can increase the morale of a group
- Are best at dealing with angry or difficult people

Weaknesses Associated With Very High Scores or Stressful Situations

- Often are late to appointments or miss work and deadlines
- Are easily bored and distracted
- Have trouble getting to the point (ramble)
- Have a tendency to gossip

Soothers

General Personality

Soothers are individuals who are calm and steady and whose greatest strength is their ability to get along with a variety of people. Soothers tend to be warm, caring people who are very loyal to their friends and their organization. Soothers enjoy stability and thus tend to keep the same friends and jobs for long periods of time. Interestingly, some evidence provided by counseling psychologists suggests that Soothers are the least likely personality type to get a divorce. Soothers tend to make excellent counselors, and if they have a high score on Thinking, also tend to be excellent computer programmers.

Soothers most fear conflict and will do almost anything to avoid it. Thus, they are inclined to allow others to take advantage of them because they will not confront others. Soothers are the most likely personality type to develop ulcers, especially if they are working with a Director. Soothers tend to set low goals for themselves, are responsive to praise, and are easily hurt by criticism.

Communication Style

Soothers communicate in a positive fashion with just about everyone. They seldom criticize others and don't want to hear others criticize them. Soothers are the most sensitive about picking up nonverbal cues and emotional states in others. They tend to listen more for the way in which things are said than for what is actually said. Soothers seldom yell, and they react poorly to those who yell at others.

Leadership Style

Soothers seldom seek leadership positions but do occasionally find themselves in leadership roles because they are good compromise candidates. That is, because they seldom have enemies, it is difficult to find a person who dislikes a Soother. When they are thrust into leadership roles, they lead by delegating work to others and then providing the emotional support necessary to complete the project. Soothers utilize a participatory leadership style in which they solicit the opinions of others before making decisions.

Strengths

- Are loyal and trusted
- Are good listeners
- Are well liked and seldom have enemies
- Are good followers, team players, and group members

Weaknesses Associated With Very High Scores or Stressful Situations

- Have difficulty making tough decisions involving people
- Tend to avoid confrontation
- Often deny that problems exist
- Are often walked on

Organizers

General Personality

Organizers are detailed, organized individuals who are more concerned with quality than with quantity. Because Organizers are perfectionists who want everything done perfectly or not done at all, they produce high-quality work. As their name implies, Organizers' greatest strength is their ability to organize people and things; they have a system for everything. Because Organizers are so compulsive, they tend to be critical of others. Due also to their love of detail, Organizers usually would rather work with data than with people.

Organizers believe in the system and in authority. They follow rules, create new regulations and policies, and expect others to also believe in and follow the system. Organizers are hard workers who do what it takes to get a job done properly. Organizers are on time to appointments and expect others to be as well. Unlike Thinkers and Communicators, Organizers enjoy carrying out the details of ideas; they are doers rather than talkers or thinkers.

Communication Style

Organizers communicate with others in a detailed, factual manner. They don't want to chit-chat, and they don't want general ideas. They are basically the Jack Webbs of the world in that they prefer "just the facts." Organizers are poor at noticing nonverbal cues and can be even worse at understanding the real meaning behind what is being said. They pay attention only to the details of the conversation.

Leadership Style

Organizers lead by organization and strategy. They have an uncanny ability to take the knowledge and resources of others and organize them so that a task can be accomplished. Like Soothers, Organizers tend to delegate authority but demand that things be done "by the book."

Strengths

- Have strong organizational skills
- Are good risk managers
- Understand the process
- Produce high-quality work

Weaknesses Associated With Very High Scores or Stressful Situations
- Have difficulty seeing the big picture
- Are resistant to change
- Are overly critical
- Are often inflexible

Exercise 5.5
Interest Inventories

In this exercise, you will get to take a shortened version of the Aamodt Vocational Interest Survey (AVIS). The AVIS is used for adult employees who are thinking about changing careers.

Directions

For each of the activities on the next two pages, rate the extent to which you might enjoy performing the activity often or for long periods of time. On the AVIS answer sheet, rate each statement using the following scale:

1   I would absolutely hate doing this activity
2   I would dislike doing this activity
3   I would neither dislike nor like doing this activity (I'm neutral)
4   I would enjoy doing this activity
5   I would very much enjoy doing this activity

Questions

1. Filing patients' charts in alphabetical order
2. Calming an angry customer
3. Testing blood samples for the presence of disease
4. Appraising the value of real estate
5. Calling people to determine their interest in a product
6. Raising livestock
7. Driving a bus
8. Overhauling an engine
9. Arresting a drug dealer
10. Caring for patients in a hospital
11. Evaluating the performance of an employee
12. Baking bread at a deli
13. Creating an advertising campaign

14. Entering information into a computer
15. Helping customers make travel arrangements
16. Taking x-rays of an injured foot
17. Predicting the success of stocks and bonds
18. Selling automobiles at a car lot
19. Planting vegetables
20. Picking up passengers in a cab
21. Repairing a broken VCR
22. Giving first aid and CPR in an emergency situation
23. Teaching young people a topic in your favorite area
24. Making tough decisions
25. Sewing clothing
26. Writing a computer program

27. Typing letters and reports
28. Answering questions about products or services
29. Cleaning teeth
30. Appraising the value of a damaged car
31. Asking people to donate money to charity
32. Baling hay
33. Delivering packages to stores
34. Fixing leaks in household plumbing
35. Driving an ambulance through the streets at a high speed
36. Helping people with marital problems
37. Setting production goals
38. Cleaning hotel rooms
39. Designing a floral arrangement

40. Sorting mail
41. Ringing up merchandise on a cash register
42. Testing urine samples for the presence of drugs
43. Determining ways to reduce a client's taxes
44. Calling people to determine their interest in selling their home
45. Plowing a field
46. Driving through heavy traffic
47. Building a house
48. Explaining crime prevention techniques to citizens
49. Working with a physically disabled person
50. Organizing daily work activities
51. Cooking meals at a nice restaurant
52. Playing a musical instrument

53. Scheduling appointments for a business executive
54. Solving customers' problems
55. Filling prescriptions at a pharmacy
56. Forecasting the economy
57. Selling products at a department store
58. Spreading fertilizer over a field
59. Parking cars in a parking garage
60. Assembling electronic components
61. Writing a ticket for a speeding motorist
62. Taking care of young children
63. Setting up employee work schedules
64. Shortening the length of a skirt
65. Coming up with ideas for a new product

AVIS Answer Sheet

(1) absolutely hate (2) dislike (3) neutral (4) enjoy (5) very much enjoy

Row Total

1. ____	14. ____	27. ____	40. ____	53. ____	____ C
2. ____	15. ____	28. ____	41. ____	54. ____	____ CS
3. ____	16. ____	29. ____	42. ____	55. ____	____ Sc
4. ____	17. ____	30. ____	43. ____	56. ____	____ A
5. ____	18. ____	31. ____	44. ____	57. ____	____ Sa
6. ____	19. ____	32. ____	45. ____	58. ____	____ Ag
7. ____	20. ____	33. ____	46. ____	59. ____	____ Tran
8. ____	21. ____	34. ____	47. ____	60. ____	____ Trd
9. ____	22. ____	35. ____	48. ____	61. ____	____ P
10. ____	23. ____	36. ____	49. ____	62. ____	____ HC
11. ____	24. ____	37. ____	50. ____	63. ____	____ LM
12. ____	25. ____	38. ____	51. ____	64. ____	____ CE
13. ____	26. ____	39. ____	52. ____	65. ____	____ Cr

AVIS Profile Sheet

Interest Area	Low Interest																				High Interest
Clerical	5	6	7	8	9	10	11	12	13	14	15	16	17	18	19	20	21	22	23	24	25
Customer Service	5	6	7	8	9	10	11	12	13	14	15	16	17	18	19	20	21	22	23	24	25
Science	5	6	7	8	9	10	11	12	13	14	15	16	17	18	19	20	21	22	23	24	25
Analysis	5	6	7	8	9	10	11	12	13	14	15	16	17	18	19	20	21	22	23	24	25
Sales	5	6	7	8	9	10	11	12	13	14	15	16	17	18	19	20	21	22	23	24	25
Agriculture	5	6	7	8	9	10	11	12	13	14	15	16	17	18	19	20	21	22	23	24	25
Transportation	5	6	7	8	9	10	11	12	13	14	15	16	17	18	19	20	21	22	23	24	25
Trades	5	6	7	8	9	10	11	12	13	14	15	16	17	18	19	20	21	22	23	24	25
Protective	5	6	7	8	9	10	11	12	13	14	15	16	17	18	19	20	21	22	23	24	25
Helping/Caring	5	6	7	8	9	10	11	12	13	14	15	16	17	18	19	20	21	22	23	24	25
Leadership/Management	5	6	7	8	9	10	11	12	13	14	15	16	17	18	19	20	21	22	23	24	25
Consumer Economics	5	6	7	8	9	10	11	12	13	14	15	16	17	18	19	20	21	22	23	24	25
Creative	5	6	7	8	9	10	11	12	13	14	15	16	17	18	19	20	21	22	23	24	25

Career Areas

Clerical
- Health Care — medical insurance clerk, medical records clerk, medical secretary, medical transcriptionist, admissions clerk
- Banking — credit clerk, mortgage clerk, loan interviewer, teller
- Hospitality — hotel clerk, ticket agent, reservation clerk
- Legal — court reporter, legal secretary, paralegal
- Office — administrative assistant, clerk, mail clerk, payroll clerk, secretary
- Manufacturing — stock clerk, shipping and receiving clerk
- Transportation — toll collector, dispatcher

Customer Service
- Health Care — dental assistant, collections, hospital insurance representative
- Banking — teller, loan officer, collections, customer service representative
- Hospitality — server, caterer, bartender, dietician, dietician's assistant
- Office — operator, switchboard, receptionist, personnel assistant
- Cosmetology — hair stylist, manicurist, barber
- Retail — cashier, sales representative, customer service representative
- Travel — travel agent, flight attendant

Science
- Dental — dental technician, dental hygienist
- Medical — medical technologist, radiographer, sonographer
- Optical — optician, optical lab technician, lens grinder
- Pharmacy — pharmacist, pharmacy assistant
- Science — lab technician
- Veterinary — veterinarian, veterinary assistant

Analysis
- Accounting — accountant, bookkeeper, financial analyst, economist
- Insurance — insurance appraiser, claims adjuster, underwriter
- Investments — financial planner, stock broker
- Law — lawyer, paralegal
- Real estate — real estate appraiser

Sales
- Aggressive — insurance, fundraiser, manufacturer's representative
- Real Estate — real estate agent, real estate broker
- Retail — sales representative, demonstrator
- Telemarketing — telemarketer

Agriculture
- Farming
- Ranching

Transportation
- Public — bus driver, cab driver, chauffeur, car lot attendant
- Delivery — delivery truck driver
- Long Haul — truck driver, escort driver

Trades
- Construction — painter, mason, asphalt paver, heavy equipment operator, carpet layer
- Electrical — electrician, electronic repairer, appliance repairer, cable installer, office machine repairer, vending machine repairer
- Mechanical — automotive mechanic, truck mechanic, maintenance mechanic, aircraft mechanic, boat mechanic
- Metal — welder, sheet metal worker
- Physical Labor — logger, miner, jackhammer operator
- Plumbing — plumber
- Production — assembler, solderer, machinist, foundry worker
- Wood — cabinetmaker, carpenter, woodworker, furniture assembler
- Other — locksmith

Protective
- Dispatch — police dispatcher, 911 operator
- Emergency — EMT, paramedic
- Fire Science — firefighter
- Outdoor — lifeguard, park ranger, fish and game warden
- Police Science — police officer, security guard

Helping/Caring
- Day Care — babysitter, child care, home companion
- Health Care — nurse, nurse's aide, physician's assistant
- Banking/Finance — loan counselor, financial counselor
- Education — teacher, teacher's aide, special education teacher
- Law — parole officer
- Outdoor — camp counselor
- Social Services — social worker, psychologist, counselor

Management
- Education — principal
- Hospitality — hotel manager, restaurant manager
- Office — office manager, personnel director
- Production — supervisor
- Retail — store manager, assistant manager

Consumer Economics
- Cooking — baker, caterer, cook, chef, dietitian, nutritionist
- Housekeeping — janitor, maid
- Textiles — tailor, sewing machine operator, weaver, dry cleaner

Creative
- Art — painter, sculptor
- Business — advertising, marketing
- Computers — computer programmer, graphic artist
- Fashion — fashion design, fashion buyer
- Floral — floral design
- Oral — actor/actress, trainer, teacher, disc jockey, broadcaster
- Outdoor — landscaper
- Photography — photographer
- Retail — jeweler
- Writing — writer, poet, technical writer, reporter

Exercise 5.6
Integrity Testing

In this chapter you learned that integrity testing has increased in popularity. This exercise will give you a chance to take a sample integrity test. Because of the sensitive nature of these tests, you will not actually receive a test score.

sd=strongly disagree   d=disagree   n=neutral   a=agree   sa=strongly agree

1. Everyone is dishonest at times.   sd d n a sa
2. Most people have stolen things from their employer.   sd d n a sa
3. Most employees in restaurants steal food.   sd d n a sa
4. Dishonesty is just part of life.   sd d n a sa
5. Most police officers would take a bribe.   sd d n a sa

6. I have stolen things from an employer.   sd d n a sa
7. I often do not tell the truth.   sd d n a sa
8. I have shoplifted in the past five years.   sd d n a sa
9. I have changed the price tag on an item I wanted to buy.   sd d n a sa
10. I have given a discount to a friend when I shouldn't have. sd d n a sa

11. I have been tempted to steal from my employer.   sd d n a sa
12. On occasion I have been tempted to shoplift.   sd d n a sa
13. There have been times when I thought about stealing.   sd d n a sa
14. I have cheated on exams in school.   sd d n a sa
15. I have lied to my friends.   sd d n a sa

16. People who steal from an employer should be fired.   sd d n a sa
17. People who shoplift should spend time in jail.   sd d n a sa
18. Stores should always file charges against shoplifters.   sd d n a sa
19. Students who cheat on exams should be suspended.   sd d n a sa
20. Punishment will not deter people from stealing.   sd d n a sa

21. It is easy to shoplift without getting caught.   sd d n a sa
22. My employer would never notice if I took a few things.   sd d n a sa
23. Very few people who steal get caught.   sd d n a sa
24. Very few students who cheat get caught.   sd d n a sa
25. People who steal might get arrested but they won't go to jail. sd d n a sa

26. My friends shoplift.   sd d n a sa
27. My friends steal things from their employer.   sd d n a sa
28. I have friends who have been arrested.   sd d n a sa
29. Most people I know have been in trouble with the law.   sd d n a sa
30. My parents are not very honest.   sd d n a sa

31. It is OK to steal from someone who has treated you poorly. sd d n a sa
32. It is OK to steal food if your family is hungry.   sd d n a sa
33. If a store clerk gives you too much change, it is OK to keep it. sd d n a sa
34. Stealing is always wrong.   sd d n a sa
35. Stealing is OK if done for the right reason.   sd d n a sa

1. What aspects of honesty do you think the sample integrity questions were measuring?

_____
_____
_____
_____
_____
_____
_____
_____

2. Do you think integrity tests should be used? Why or why not?

_____
_____
_____
_____
_____
_____
_____
_____

3. Do you think you could successfully fake an integrity test? Are the questions so obvious that applicants will know how to answer the questions in order to pass the test?

_____
_____
_____

Exercise 5.7
Resume Evaluation

On the next page is a resume of an applicant for an assistant manager position. On the basis of this person's resume, would you hire him? Why or why not?

xxxxxx
8213 Summerdale Avenue
Chicago, IL 60610

Job Objective
    Supervisory or management position with a progressive organization

Professional Strengths
- Extensive management experience
- Award-winning sales and promotional skills
- Active in the community
- Excellent construction, remodeling, and maintenance skills

Professional Experience

Owner - PDM Contractors - Chicago, Illinois
    Owned and operated a successful general contracting and remodeling business. Responsibilities included bidding for jobs; supervising construction and remodeling; hiring, scheduling, and supervising employees; and handling all financial and accounting duties.

Manager - Kentucky Fried Chicken - Waterloo, Iowa
    Responsible for managing three KFC restaurants. High level of performance demonstrated by huge increases in store profits.

Management Trainee - Nunn-Bush Shoes - Springfield, Illinois
    Responsibilities included hiring, scheduling, and supervising employees; maintaining inventory; and selling shoes. High level of performance led to several promotions and commendations.

Ambulance Attendant - Palm Mortuary - Las Vegas, Nevada

Grocery Bagger - IGA - Chicago, Illinois

Community Activities
    Waterloo, Iowa
- Named "Best Jaycee Chaplain" in Iowa
- Member of the Merchant Patrol

    Springfield, Illinois
- Vice president of the Jaycees
- Ran largest Christmas parade in central Illinois
- Named *Outstanding First Year Jaycee* and *Third Outstanding Jaycee Member* in Illinois
- Member Junior Chamber of Commerce

    Chicago, Illinois
- Precinct Captain for the Democratic Party
- Member, St. John Berchmans' parish bowling team
- Organizer of annual Snowtillion (church winter dance)
- Directed the annual Polish Constitution Day Parade
- Member of the Moose Lodge

Education
    Diploma
Northwestern Business College

Exercise 6.1
Locating Test Information

You are the personnel assistant for a large corporation. The company I/O psychologist has just completed a job analysis of some supervisory positions and is now looking for tests that will tap the knowledge, skills, and abilities identified in the job analysis. The I/O psychologist has asked you to find information about two types of tests: a math test and a personality test that measures extroversion.

Use the test compendia discussed in the text to do the following:

1) Identify potential tests to use

2) List the reliability of each test

3) List the cost of each test

4) List the administration time for each test

Math Test

Test Name	Reliability	Cost	Administration Time

Personality Test (Extraversion)

Test Name	Reliability	Cost	Administration Time

Exercise 6.2
Using the Utility Formula and Tables

Instructions

Below you will find a description of a hypothetical employment situation. Use the information to determine how much money your organization will save if it adopts the proposed selection test.

Situation

You have 400 applicants and 200 job openings. The validity of your proposed test, the Reilly Statistical Logic Test, is .30, and the test costs $4 per applicant to administer. You have 1000 current employees, 800 of whom are satisfactory. The salary for the position is $50,000, and the typical employee stays for four years. Currently, you are using the Robson Math Test with a validity of .25 that costs $8 per applicant to administer. Be sure to show your calculations.

1. On the basis of the Taylor-Russell Tables (Table 6.4), what percentage of future employees will be successful? _____

2. Using the utility formula, how much money does your current test, the Robson Math Test, save the company over using no test at all? _____

3. Using the utility formula, how much money does your proposed test, the Reilly Statistical Logic Test, save the company over using no test at all? _____

4. How much money will your proposed test save when compared to the Robson Math Test?

   _____

What would the figures be if no validity data were available but the current method of selection was an unstructured interview costing $15 per applicant and the proposed method was a structured interview also costing $15 per applicant? (Hint: Use the observed validity coefficient for unstructured interviews found in Table 5.2 of your text.)

1. On the basis of the Taylor-Russell Tables, what percentage of future employees will be successful?
   _____

2. Using the utility formula, how much money does your current test, the unstructured interview, save the company over using no test at all? _____

3. Using the utility formula, how much money does your proposed test, the structured interview, save the company over using no test at all? _____

4. How much money will your structured interview save when compared to the unstructured interview?
   _____

Exercise 6.3
Determining the Proportion of Correct Decisions

Instructions

Below you will find two sets of numbers. The first number represents the employee's score on a selection test. Typically, the company must hire half of the applicants who apply for jobs. The second number represents the number of months the employee was employed with the company. To be considered a success, the employee must stay with the company long enough for it to recoup its recruitment and training costs. The company believes that this period is five months.

Use the data to complete the chart on the following page to determine the proportion of correct decisions that will be made if the company decides to use the test in the future.

Test Score	Tenure
2	4
6	7
9	9
8	6
3	2
7	3
1	4
9	7
4	4
4	6
8	8
2	7
4	5
6	4
4	3
6	6
3	1
4	7
7	6
8	7

	9	-	-	-	-	-	-	-	-	-
	8	-	-	-	-	-	-	-	-	-
	7	-	-	-	-	-	-	-	-	-
T	6	-	-	-	-	-	-	-	-	-
E										
N	5	-	-	-	-	-	-	-	-	-
U	4	-	-	-	-	-	-	-	-	-
R										
E	3	-	-	-	-	-	-	-	-	-
	2	-	-	-	-	-	-	-	-	-
	1	-	-	-	-	-	-	-	-	-
		1	2	3	4	5	6	7	8	9

Test Score

Exercise 6.4
Using Banding to Reduce Adverse Impact

You are the human resource manager for the law firm of Lie, Cheat, and Steele. On the basis of your most recent employment figures, you would like to hire more female attorneys. You have four openings, and the results of the selection exam are shown on the next page. The reliability of your selection exam is .83 and the standard deviation is 7.43. On the basis of the data, do the following:

1. Compute the standard error.

2. Determine the width of a band using a 95% confidence interval (1.96 x the standard error).

3. If you used a non-sliding band, which four applicants would you hire?

_____   _____

_____   _____

4. If you used a sliding band, which four applicants would you hire?

_____   _____

_____   _____

5. If you used a passing score of 80 rather than a band, what four applicants would you hire?

_____   _____

_____   _____

Applicants to the Law Firm of Lie, Cheat, and Steele

2009 Test Scores

Applicant	Score	Gender
Jack McCoy	97	m
Denny Crane	95	m
Paul Robinette	94	m
Adam Schiff	94	m
Abbie Carmichael	91	f
Ron Carver	89	m
Jamie Ross	89	f
Michael Cutter	88	m
Claire Kincaid	87	f
Alexandra Cabot	86	f
Ben Stone	86	m
Nora Lewin	85	f
Alan Shore	83	m
Arthur Branch	80	m
Carl Sack	78	m
Serena Southerlyn	70	f
Paul Lewiston	70	m
Casey Novak	68	f
Alexandra Borgia	65	f
Connie Rubirosa	65	f

Exercise 7.1
360-Degree Feedback

_____

Your text indicated that it is increasingly popular to have a variety of sources evaluate an employee's performance. This practice is called *360-degree feedback*. Imagine that you have been asked to design a 360-feedback system for servers (waiters, waitresses) in a restaurant. On the lines below, indicate what sources you would use to gather feedback.

_____
_____
_____
_____
_____
_____
_____
_____

Comments

_____
_____
_____
_____
_____
_____
_____

Exercise 7.2
Creating Performance Dimensions

Imagine that you are the HR manager for a chain of restaurants and have decided to create a performance appraisal system. Using Table 7.2 in the text as a guide, list your performance dimensions for each of the four types of dimensions. To help you, a sample dimension is already listed for each type of dimension. After writing your dimensions, decide which one you like best.

Competency-focused

Memory

Task-focused

Taking orders

Goal focused

Get food orders correct

Trait focused

Friendly

Exercise 7.3
Paired-Comparison Technique

The paired-comparison technique for ranking performance was discussed in your text. With this technique, rather than ranking several employees at one time, employees are compared one pair at a time. This exercise provides you with practice using this technique.

Step 1: List the names of the professors you have had in your last five classes. (Do not use the name of your professor in this class.)

A. _____

B. _____

C. _____

D. _____

E. _____

Step 2: Write the names of the professors in the appropriate spaces below. Once these names have been written, circle the professor in each pair that you thought was the better professor of the two.

A. _____	B. _____
A. _____	C. _____
A. _____	D. _____
A. _____	E. _____
B. _____	C. _____
B. _____	D. _____
B. _____	E. _____
C. _____	D. _____
C. _____	E. _____
D. _____	E. _____

Step 3: Count the number of times you circled each name above and place that number on the chart below.

Professor   Times Chosen

A. _____   _____

B. _____   _____

C. _____   _____

D. _____   _____

E. _____   _____

Exercise 7.4
Writing Behavioral Statements

One of the steps to creating a performance appraisal instrument is to convert the task statements from a job description into behavioral expectations. In this list of tasks performed by restaurant servers, convert each of the tasks into a behavioral expectation. The first two have been done for you to serve as examples. Note that few of your behavioral expectations will be as precise as those provided as examples. Figure 7.6 in your text can provide you with more examples.

Task	Behavioral Expectation
1. Cleans tables after customers leave	*Tables are cleaned within 2 minutes of customer leaving*
2. Gives customers menus	*Customers received menu within 3 minutes of sitting at the table*
3. Suggests appetizers	_____
4. Takes customers' drink orders	_____
5. Informs customers of specials	_____
6. Brings drinks and appetizers to customers	_____
7. Takes customers' food orders	_____
8. Places food orders with the kitchen	_____
9. Prepares salads and soups	_____
10. Brings salads and soups to customers	_____
11. Picks up salad plates and soup bowls	_____
12. Brings food to customers	_____
13. Refills customers' drinks	_____
14. Suggests appetizers and deserts	_____

Exercise 7.5
Evaluating Employee Performance

Your text discussed the use of objective data to evaluate employee performance. Below, you will find data on the number of traffic citations written by police officers. Indicate what performance rating you would give each of the officers. Select the person you think is the best officer and the person you think is the worst officer. Your instructor will discuss your ratings in class.

Officer	Traffic Citations Written	Performance Rating	
Malloy	33	_____	1 = below expectations
Reed	34	_____	2 = meets expectations
Ho	10	_____	3 = exceeds
Romano	19	_____	4 = greatly exceeds
Hooker	23	_____	
Williams	09	_____	
Boscarelli	17	_____	
Fife	14	_____	
Friday	08	_____	
Yokus	23	_____	
Taylor	15	_____	
Gannon	08	_____	
Lacey	09	_____	
Renko	04	_____	
Baker	02	_____	
Briscoe	15	_____	
Sullivan	11	_____	
Bates	12	_____	
Green	17	_____	
Davis	10	_____	
Coffey	03	_____	
Cagney	07	_____	
Hill	06	_____	
Poncherello	05	_____	

DEPARTMENT MEAN 13.04

Best officer _____   Worst officer _____

Exercise 7.6
Rating Errors

Think of four professors that you had last semester. Write down their names in the places below and then rate each professor on the five dimensions.

PROFESSOR A:_____

Knowledge of Subject	1 2 3 4 5
Fairness of Grades	1 2 3 4 5
Organization	1 2 3 4 5
Speaking Skills	1 2 3 4 5
Interest in Students	1 2 3 4 5

PROFESSOR B:_____

Knowledge of Subject	1 2 3 4 5
Fairness of Grades	1 2 3 4 5
Organization	1 2 3 4 5
Speaking Skills	1 2 3 4 5
Interest in Students	1 2 3 4 5

PROFESSOR C:_____

Knowledge of Subject	1 2 3 4 5
Fairness of Grades	1 2 3 4 5
Organization	1 2 3 4 5
Speaking Skills	1 2 3 4 5
Interest in Students	1 2 3 4 5

PROFESSOR D:_____

Knowledge of Subject	1 2 3 4 5
Fairness of Grades	1 2 3 4 5
Organization	1 2 3 4 5
Speaking Skills	1 2 3 4 5
Interest in Students	1 2 3 4 5

Once you have finished, look at the pattern of ratings that you made. Did your ratings suffer from any of the rating errors discussed in your text?

_____

_____

Exercise 7.7
Performance Appraisal Interviews

The most important aspect of the performance appraisal system is the feedback that it provides an employee. This feedback, which should improve employee performance, is usually given during the performance appraisal review. This exercise provides you with an opportunity to conduct a performance appraisal review.

Instructions

Think of the last waiter or waitress who served you at a restaurant. Once you have this person in mind, use a 5-point scale to rate the server on the dimensions you identified in the critical incident exercise (Exercise 2.4). If you have not done that exercise, do so now. Write down comments about specific good and bad behaviors that you saw this server perform.

Pair up with another member of your class and pretend that you are the restaurant owner and the student is actually your server. Using the knowledge you obtained from your text, conduct the performance appraisal interview with your classmate posing as the server. When you have completed your interview, switch roles and let your classmate conduct his/her interview with you.

What did you do in the performance appraisal interview? How did the "server" react to what you did and said? What could you do to improve the review?

Exercise 8.1
Needs Assessment: Task Analysis

Below you will find part of a job description for a part-time position in a campus bookstore. Read each task in the job description and identify those tasks for which training (rather than employee selection techniques) would be appropriate. In the next exercise, you will be asked to determine how to train the employees for each of the tasks you identify.

Textbook Clerk

Job Summary

The Textbook Clerk is a university work-study position. The student hired for this job is responsible for assisting the Textbook Supervisor with book inventories, shelving duties, and customer requests. Additionally, the Textbook Clerk performs general clerical and messenger duties and operates the cash register when additional assistance is needed.

Work Activities

Inventory Duties

- Inventories books by section and course number
- Informs supervisor of number of books to be returned
- Writes ISBN on inventory sheet
- Verifies all information as typed on each textbook requisition
- Records price information

Shelving Duties

- Shelves returned books
- Straightens shelves
- Removes previous semester's textbooks from store shelves at the end of each semester
- Shelves used books in the stockroom by title
- Shelves new books in the stockroom by publisher
- Places typed shelf cards on appropriate shelf
- Dusts shelves
- Dusts books

Customer Relations Duties

- Phones professors regarding new textbook editions
- Mails book arrival notices to professors

Clerical Duties

- Types shelf cards
- Types book arrival notices
- Types PU-6 Forms
- Photocopies book orders and notices about book arrivals

Messenger Duties

- Delivers materials or messages to other employees
- Delivers materials to university departments

Cash Register Duties

- Writes name on register tab at beginning and end of shift
- Watches customers entering store to make sure they do not take books and backpacks into store
- Tabulates price of purchases using cash register
- Counts appropriate change and gives it to customers
- Pages employee on register list to assist with checkout when lines are long
- Approves student's checks by validating university ID or by certifying driver's license
- Approves out-of-town checks by verifying name, address, and phone number with driver's license
- Pages supervisor to fill out void slips
- Completes in-slip forms for returns
- Sells laundry tickets, computer disks, and dissection coupons to students
- Verifies textbook tags for price and author codes to ensure that the correct tag is still on the textbook
- Pages supervisor if tag and code are incorrect

Exercise 8.2
Needs Assessment: Person Analysis

On the next page, you will find sample performance appraisal data for 10 employees at a bank. A rating of 1 is considered poor, 3 is satisfactory, and 5 is excellent. Due to budget constraints, we want to train any employee whose performance is less than satisfactory. Look at the data and determine:

a) What types of training are needed for all employees?

_____

_____

_____

_____

_____

b) What training is needed by each employee?

Dawson   _____

Anderson   _____

Barker   _____

Trebek   _____

Sajak   _____

Marshall   _____

Eubanks   _____

Cullen   _____

Clark   _____

Ludden   _____

	Performance Dimension						
Employee	A	B	C	D	E	F	G
Dawson	5	2	3	5	5	2	5
Anderson	4	5	1	5	5	4	1
Barker	5	4	4	5	5	5	3
Trebek	5	5	2	4	5	4	5
Sajak	5	4	2	5	5	1	4
Marshall	5	2	2	5	5	5	5
Eubanks	4	5	4	5	5	2	4
Cullen	4	5	1	3	5	3	4
Clark	4	1	1	2	1	3	2
Ludden	5	4	3	5	5	1	2

Note: A rating of 5 indicates excellent performance.

A = Accuracy of Data Input
B = Accuracy of Teller Drawer
C = Cross-Selling
D = Friendliness
E = Attendance
F = Knowledge of Bank Services
G = Knowledge of Customer Names

Exercise 8.3
Evaluating Training Programs: 1

As training director for Beavis Enterprises, you are constantly "butting heads" with the other division directors about the need for training. To show the division heads the importance of training, you decide to conduct an experiment. Half of your employees attend a workshop in which information about the company product is presented. The other half, do not receive this training. All employees are monitored before the training period on the percentage of correct information they provide to customers and then monitored again 3 weeks after the training program is completed.

On the basis of the data from the following page, did your training program work? In the space below, justify your answer. You might want to draw a chart or table to best represent your findings.

Employee	Training Condition	Pretest Score	Posttest Score
Hofstadter	no training	68	73
Cooper	training	79	86
Wolowitz	training	62	73
Penny	no training	83	82
Koothrappali	no training	63	67
Winkle	training	77	84
Crane	training	61	75
Moon	no training	74	74
Doyle	training	84	84
Truman	training	68	70
Adler	no training	70	79
Walker	training	53	58
McFarland	no training	79	88
Heffernan	training	54	71
Spooner	training	93	90
Palmer	no training	71	76
Olchin	no training	76	78
Becker	no training	88	89
Kostas	training	88	92
Wyborn	no training	67	80
Malinak	training	74	80
Hughley	training	64	67
Milsap	no training	61	75
Rogers	training	71	72
Carey	no training	64	73
Lewis	training	85	86
Bobeck	training	70	75
O'Brien	no training	69	68
Oswald	no training	72	79
Wick	no training	68	74

Exercise 8.4
Evaluating Training Programs: 2

In an attempt to increase the performance of its customer service employees, the Clinton Whitewater Canoe Company recently conducted a new training program. The training program involved a series of lectures and discussions to reduce the number of complaints made by customers purchasing a new canoe.

Before spending thousands of dollars on the training, the company allowed three different outside trainers the opportunity to each conduct a training session, with the idea being that the company would then offer a contract to the trainer doing the best job.

On the next page, you will find data for the three training sessions. The effectiveness of the training was evaluated through employee ratings of the trainer, a test of customer service knowledge following training, and the number of customer complaints received by the employee in the 2 weeks following the training session.

The instructor rating was made on a 5-point scale (a rating of 5 is excellent and a rating of 1 is poor) and represents how well the employees thought the trainer conducted the training session. The test score is the percentage of items that each employee got correct on the test of customer service knowledge.

As director of training, your job is to use the data on the next page to make a recommendation about which trainer should be offered the training contract. Justify your reasoning below (hint: you might want to create a chart to help make your decision).

_____

_____

_____

_____

_____

_____

_____

_____

Employee	Trainer	Instructor Rating	Test Score	Customer Complaints
Brooks	Leno	4	71	2
Byrd	Leno	5	78	2
Carpenter	Leno	5	83	3
Dunn	Leno	5	75	2
Hill	Leno	5	94	1
McGraw	Leno	5	97	2
Pickler	Leno	4	80	1
Rimes	Leno	4	82	3
Swift	Leno	5	72	2
Twain	Leno	4	74	1
Bennet	Carson	3	84	2
Cole	Carson	3	81	1
Clooney	Carson	3	84	1
Crosby	Carson	2	78	2
Goulet	Carson	3	88	3
Martin	Carson	3	83	2
Mathis	Carson	5	85	1
Newton	Carson	3	80	0
Sinatra	Carson	3	93	1
Williams	Carson	4	98	1
Aguilera	Parr	5	81	0
Archuleta	Parr	4	77	1
Blige	Parr	3	82	1
Carey	Parr	3	72	0
Dayne	Parr	3	77	0
Houston	Parr	4	84	1
Keys	Parr	5	85	0
Knowles	Parr	4	73	1
LaBelle	Parr	3	81	1
Turner	Parr	4	79	2

Exercise 9.1
Focused Free-Write – Motivation

Describe a job (or a class) you have had in which you were very motivated to perform well. Why do you think you were so motivated?

Now describe a job (or class) in which you were not motivated to perform well. Why?

Exercise 9.2
Self-Esteem

The Radford Self-Esteem Inventory

Here is a list of statements about feelings. For each statement, place an "X" in the appropriate column to indicate the extent to which you agree with the statement.

	Strongly disagree	disagree	neutral	agree	Strongly agree
1. Difficult situations usually don't bother me.	1	2	3	4	5
2. I don't like a lot of things about me.	5	4	3	2	1
3. I have good ideas.	1	2	3	4	5
4. I have a low opinion of myself.	5	4	3	2	1
5. I like trying new things.	1	2	3	4	5
6. I am a confident person.	1	2	3	4	5
7. I am not afraid to take risks.	1	2	3	4	5
8. I do most things well.	1	2	3	4	5
9. I am happy with who I am.	1	2	3	4	5
10. I am a likeable person.	1	2	3	4	5
11. There is not much about my personality that I would change.	1	2	3	4	5
12. I am successful at almost everything I try.	1	2	3	4	5
13. I am a good person.	1	2	3	4	5
14. I have a lot of respect for myself.	1	2	3	4	5
15. I am comfortable with who I am.	1	2	3	4	5
16. There is little I cannot accomplish if I set my mind to it.	1	2	3	4	5
17. I am a talented person.	1	2	3	4	5
18. I can overcome any obstacles in my life.	1	2	3	4	5
19. I am as good a person as anyone.	1	2	3	4	5
20. There are so many people I would rather be than me.	5	4	3	2	1

Scoring and Interpreting the Radford Inventory

The Radford Inventory measures your level of self-esteem. To score the inventory, add the points that correspond to the choices you made for each question.

Your self-esteem score is _____.

To interpret your score, look at the chart below and circle where your scores fall.

	Self-Worth
Top 20%	82 - 100
Next 20%	78 - 81
Middle 20%	75 - 77
Next 20%	68 - 74
Bottom 20%	20 - 67

On the basis of what you learned about consistency theory, how motivated would your self-esteem score suggest that you would be?

_____

_____

_____

_____

_____

Exercise 9.3
Intrinsic Versus Extrinsic Motivation

Work Preference Inventory (College Student Version; Copyright 1987, Teresa M. Amabile, used with permission of the author.)

Please rate each item in terms of how true it is of you. Please circle one and only one letter for each question according to the following scale:

> N = **Never** or almost never true of you
> S = **Sometimes** true of you
> O = **Often** true of you
> A = **Always** or almost always true of you

N S O A   1. I am concerned about what other people think of my work.

N S O A   2. I prefer having someone set clear goals for me in my work.

N S O A   3. The more difficult the problem, the more I enjoy trying to solve it.

N S O A   4. I am keenly aware of the goals I have for getting good grades.

N S O A   5. I want my work to provide me with opportunities to increase my knowledge and skills.

N S O A   6. To me, success means doing better than other people.

N S O A   7. I prefer to figure things out for myself.

N S O A   8. No matter what the outcome of a project, I am satisfied if I feel I gained a new experience.

N S O A   9. I dislike relatively simple, straightforward tasks.

N S O A   10. I am keenly aware of the GPA (grade point average) goals I have for myself.

N S O A   11. Curiosity is the driving force behind much of what I do.

N S O A   12. I'm less concerned with what work I do than what I get for it.

N S O A   13. I enjoy tackling problems that are completely new to me.

N S O A   14. I prefer work that stretches my abilities over work I know I can do well.

N S O A   15. I'm concerned about how other people are going to react to my ideas.

N S O A   16. I often think about grades and awards.

N   S   O   A   17. I'm more comfortable when I can set my own goals.

N   S   O   A   18. I believe that there is no point in doing a good job if nobody else knows about it.

N   S   O   A   19. I am strongly motivated by the grades I can earn.

N   S   O   A   20. It is important to me to be able to do what I enjoy most.

N   S   O   A   21. I prefer working on projects with clearly specified procedures.

N   S   O   A   22. As long as I can do what I enjoy, I'm not that concerned about exactly what grades or awards I earn.

N   S   O   A   23. I enjoy doing work that is so absorbing that I forget about everything else.

N   S   O   A   24. I am strongly motivated by the recognition I can earn from others.

N   S   O   A   25. I have to feel that I'm earning something for what I do.

N   S   O   A   26. I enjoy trying to solve complex problems.

N   S   O   A   27. It is important for me to have an outlet for self-expression.

N   S   O   A   28. I want to find out how good I really can be at my work.

N   S   O   A   29. I want other people to find out how good I really can be at my work.

N   S   O   A   30. What matters most to me is enjoying what I do.

Interpreting the Work Preference Inventory

The Work Preference Inventory was developed by Dr. Teresa Amabile and measures your predisposition to be intrinsically and extrinsically motivated. To score the WPI, give yourself 1 point if you circled an "N," 2 points if you circled an "S," 3 points if you circled an "O," and 4 points if you circled an "A."

To determine your level of intrinsic motivation, add your points for Questions 3, 5, 7, 8, 9, 11, 13, 14, 17, 20, 23, 26, 27, 28, and 30. _____

To determine your level of extrinsic motivation, add your points for Questions 1, 2, 4, 6, 10, 12, 15, 16, 18, 19, 21, 24, 25, and 29. _____ On question 22 reverse your score (A = 1, O = 2, S = 3, and N =1), and add this score to the total for the other 14 questions. _____

To interpret your score, look at the chart below and circle where your scores fall. Are you an intrinsically or extrinsically motivated person?

	Intrinsic Motivation	Extrinsic Motivation
Top 20%	46 - 60	43 - 60
Next 20%	45 - 47	39 - 42
Middle 20%	43 - 44	37 - 38
Next 20%	40 - 42	35 - 36
Bottom 20%	15 - 39	15 - 34

On the basis of what you read in the text, what does your score on the WPI tell you about your personal tendency toward motivation?

_____

_____

_____

_____

_____

_____

_____

_____

_____

_____

Exercise 9.4
Goal Setting

Your text discussed the value of goal setting as a way to improve employee performance. However, goal setting works in many settings outside of work. The purpose of this exercise is to provide you with the opportunity to use your knowledge of goal setting to set your academic and career goals.

In the space below, set goals for what you want to accomplish next semester as well as for the rest of your life. Once these goals have been set, indicate how you plan to reach these goals. For example, if you set a goal of getting a job that pays $30,000 a year, what are you going to do that will allow you to get this salary?

Exercise 9.5
Reinforcement Hierarchy

Chapter 9 discussed the idea that it is often difficult to reward employees because each employee values different things in life. This idea is called the Premack Principle. It is the purpose of this exercise to give you the opportunity to create your own reinforcement hierarchy.

Instructions

Think of your current job or one that you have had recently. Once you have this job in mind, create a reinforcement hierarchy for yourself. Use the example in your text as a guide.

Most Liked

1. _____
2. _____
3. _____
4. _____
5. _____
6. _____
7. _____
8. _____
9. _____
10. _____
11. _____
12. _____
13. _____
14. _____
15. _____

Least Liked

Exercise 9.6
Expectancy and Equity Theories

Instructions

Think of the job that you have now or one that you recently had. If you were in charge, how would you use the expectancy and equity theories to increase employee motivation and job satisfaction?

Exercise 9.7
Motivation Case Study

For the past 5 months, Vacua Can, a manager at Orion Manufacturing, has come home from work depressed and angry. It seems no matter what she does, she can't motivate her employees to improve their performance. Over the past year, Vacua sent each employee to an extensive training seminar, spent money on new equipment, and transferred out the employees who lacked the ability to do their jobs. Despite these interventions, her department's performance is at the same level it was 2 years ago. Because of this performance stagnation, Vacua is worried that she will be fired.

Vacua thought that a boost in morale might increase performance, so she gave each employee a 12% raise. Yet, instead of morale being increased, many employees complained even louder than before.

Vacua also held a department meeting in which she gave an inspirational appeal for everyone to "work hard and do the very best job you possibly can." Her department seemed enthusiastic for a week, but productivity did not change.

Where did Vacua Can go wrong? What advice can you give her to motivate her employees?

Exercise 9.8
Your Own Motivation Theory

In Chapter 9, you learned about many different theories for why employees are satisfied with their jobs and why they are motivated to perform well. Even though none of the theories has been completely supported, each has something to offer. On the basis of the various theories, as well as on your experiences, design your own theory of job motivation and satisfaction. Feel free to borrow as much as you want from each of the theories discussed in your text.

Exercise 10.1
Focused Free Write – Satisfaction

Describe a job (or a class) in which you were really happy. Why do you think you were so satisfied?

Now describe a job (or class) in which you were not happy or satisfied. Why did you feel this way?

Exercise 10.2
Stability of Job Satisfaction

In the space below, write down all of the jobs you have had. Then rate the extent to which you were satisfied with each of those jobs. Are your ratings consistent? Do your ratings support the idea that job satisfaction is consistent across jobs?

VD = very dissatisfied D = dissatisfied N = neutral S = satisfied VS = Very satisfied

Job	Level of Job Satisfaction
_____	VD D N S VS
_____	VD D N S VS
_____	VD D N S VS
_____	VD D N S VS
_____	VD D N S VS
_____	VD D N S VS

_____

_____

_____

_____

_____

_____

_____

_____

Exercise 10.3
Core Self-Evaluation

Circle the number corresponding to the extent to which you agree with each of the following statements.

sd = strongly disagree
d = disagree
n = neutral
a = agree
sa = strongly agree

		sd	d	n	a	sa
1.	Difficult situations usually don't bother me.	1	2	3	4	5
2.	I don't like a lot of things about me.	5	4	3	2	1
3.	I have good ideas.	1	2	3	4	5
4.	I worry a lot.	5	4	3	2	1
5.	I have a low opinion of myself.	5	4	3	2	1
6.	I like trying new things.	1	2	3	4	5
7.	Life is fun.	1	2	3	4	5
8.	If I work hard, I will be successful.	1	2	3	4	5
9.	I don't seem to be able to control my life.	5	4	3	2	1
10.	I am a confident person.	1	2	3	4	5
11.	It seems as if my life is controlled by everyone but me.	5	4	3	2	1
12.	I am not afraid to take risks.	1	2	3	4	5
13.	I do most things well.	1	2	3	4	5
14.	People would describe me as being anxious.	5	4	3	2	1
15.	I am happy with who I am.	1	2	3	4	5
16.	I handle pressure well.	1	2	3	4	5
17.	I am successful at most things I try.	1	2	3	4	5
18.	I am usually in a good mood.	1	2	3	4	5
19.	I am a good person.	1	2	3	4	5
20.	I have a lot of respect for myself.	1	2	3	4	5
21.	I am as good a person as anybody.	1	2	3	4	5
22.	I can overcome any obstacles in my life.	1	2	3	4	5
23.	There is not much I worry about.	1	2	3	4	5
24.	I am comfortable with who I am.	1	2	3	4	5
25.	People who work hard will succeed.	1	2	3	4	5
26.	I am responsible for my success and failure	1	2	3	4	5
27.	I get depressed a lot.	5	4	3	2	1
28.	I am often nervous.	5	4	3	2	1
29.	I control my own destiny.	1	2	3	4	5
30.	I am a talented person.	1	2	3	4	5
31.	I am a likeable person.	1	2	3	4	5
32.	Others would describe me as being enthusiastic.	1	2	3	4	5
33.	There are so many people I would rather be than me.	5	4	3	2	1
34.	There is little I cannot accomplish if I set my mind to it.	1	2	3	4	5
35.	Most of what happens in life is uncontrollable.	5	4	3	2	1
36.	There is not much about my personality that I would change.	1	2	3	4	5

Scoring and Interpreting the Core Evaluation Inventory

Add the numbers associated with the answers you circled for each question.

Your total score is _____. The higher your score, the greater your predisposition to be satisfied at work and in life. The chart that follows will help you compare your score to those of other college students.

If your score was	Your core self-evaluation is higher than ____ of other college students
164-180	99%
160-163	95%
156-159	90%
153-155	85%
150-152	80%
147-149	75%
143-146	70%
142	65%
141	60%
140	55%
139	50%
138	45%
137	40%
136	35%
134-135	30%
132-133	25%
129-131	20%
123-128	15%
119-121	10%
115-118	5%
<115	<5%

Exercise 10.4
Your Level of Life Satisfaction

Circle the number next to each question that best indicates how you currently feel.

		Not at all like me				Very much like me
1.	My life situation is better than most people's.	1	2	3	4	5
2.	Most days I am very happy.	1	2	3	4	5
3.	I seldom get depressed these days.	1	2	3	4	5
4.	There is not much about my life that I want to change.	1	2	3	4	5
5.	The world is treating me pretty well.	1	2	3	4	5
6.	Things seem to be going my way.	1	2	3	4	5
7.	At my current age, I am about where I want to be in life.	1	2	3	4	5
8.	If I could relive the last few months, there is very little that I would change.	1	2	3	4	5
9.	My thoughts are usually very positive.	1	2	3	4	5
10.	I don't see how my life could get much better.	1	2	3	4	5

Scoring the Life Satisfaction Inventory

Add the numbers that you circled for each question and write that number here _____.

For example, if you had circled the bold-faced numbers in the three questions below, your total would be 7 (2 + 3 + 2).

2.	Most days I am very happy.	1	**2**	3	4	5
3.	I seldom get depressed these days.	1	2	**3**	4	5
4.	There is not much about my life that I want to change.	1	**2**	3	4	5

Interpreting the Life Satisfaction Inventory

If your score was	Your level of life satisfaction is better than ____ of other college students
49	99%
47-48	95%
45-46	90%
44	85%
43	80%
42	75%
41	70%
40	65%
39	60%
38	55%
37	45%
36	40%
35	30%
34	25%
33	20%
31-32	15%
29-30	10%
27-28	5%
<27	<5%

Exercise 10.5
Case Study

Juan Estoban was eating lunch at Anderson's Restaurant one Thursday when he noticed a help-wanted ad for the restaurant on his placemat. The ad indicated that most servers made more than $20 an hour and that the restaurant atmosphere was fun, exciting, and a place to meet new friends. As a college student, Juan thought the job opportunity was perfect: The money was good, and because most of his friends were back in Arizona, the chance to have a good time and make new friends was highly appealing.

During his job interview, the restaurant manager promised Juan that he wouldn't have to work more than 20 hours a week and that he could always have one Friday or Saturday off each week. Juan accepted the job offer and began work on the following Monday.

The first week at work was spent learning the menu, restaurant rules, and serving techniques. Juan was one of five new servers, but he was the only one who was also attending college. As one would expect, the second week was a bit stressful as the new servers began waiting tables. The first day was filled with mistakes, but by the end of the week the five new servers were performing like experts.

As the weeks passed, Juan began to fill stressed as he tried to balance his 15-hour course load with the demands of his new job. Most weeks he worked 30 hours, and he had not had a Friday or Saturday night off in the past 2 months. During the next month, Juan called in sick one Friday and then again a week later on a Saturday. Juan was also feeling a financial pinch. Even though he was working more hours than he expected, his base pay and tips averaged only around $9 an hour. Though he liked his coworkers, Juan always seemed to be arguing with his supervisor, who Juan thought was giving the best hours to employees with less seniority than he had. Even worse, the restaurant was constantly busy, and there was never any time to joke around or have fun. Juan's grades began to drop, and after failing a test in his 8:00 a.m. history class, Juan finally quit his job.

On the basis of the theories discussed in the text, what caused Juan to quit and become so dissatisfied and quit?

Exercise 10.6
Absenteeism

Your text discussed several theories about absenteeism. From these theories came several suggestions for improving attendance. The purpose of this exercise is to provide you with the opportunity to apply these theories.

Instructions

You have probably noticed throughout your college career that attendance is high in some courses and low in others. You have also probably experienced a wide variety of attendance policies. For the first part of this exercise, think of the courses you have had, and write down some of the attendance policies that you have had. Indicate next to the policy whether you thought it was effective.

For the second part of this exercise, design what you think is the ideal attendance policy for class. For every part of your plan, mention the theory or reason *discussed in the text* that supports your thinking.

Exercise 11.1
Focused Free-Write

To get you thinking about how the material in this chapter relates to your own life, think of a situation in which you and another person did not communicate effectively. Describe what happened and then indicate why you think the miscommunication took place.

Exercise 11.2
Horizontal Communication

As discussed in your text, horizontal communication is communication between employees at the same level of the organization. Some of this communication is formal, but the rest is informal and is communicated through the grapevine. The purpose of this exercise is to provide you with the opportunity to study the grapevine in your own life.

Instructions

Think of an interesting piece of information (rumor, gossip, etc.) that you have recently heard and write that information below.

_____

_____

_____

_____

Now write down the name of the person who told you that piece of information.

_____

Go to that person and ask him/her where he/she got the piece of information.

Write that name here _____.

Continue to track these people down until you come to a dead end. Also, ask each person who they told the information to.

_____

_____

_____

_____

After reaching the end, discuss the type of grapevine pattern that you found. Was it single strand, gossip, probability, or cluster? Also, how would you classify each of the people to whom you talked? Are they isolates, liaisons, or dead-enders?

_____

_____

_____

Exercise 11.3
Nonverbal Communication

Much of what is communicated is communicated nonverbally through cues such as body language, use of space, use of time, paralanguage, and artifacts. The purpose of this exercise is to provide you with the opportunity to study the extent to which nonverbal cues exist in normal conversation.

Instructions

Outside of class, go somewhere where people talk. It might be the cafeteria, the library, or a lounge in a residence hall. Quietly observe the people who are talking, and use the form below to record your observations. Write down what you saw as well as the impression you got from each of the cues.

Observation Record

Body Language

Eye Contact
_____
_____
_____

Arms
_____
_____
_____

Legs
_____
_____
_____

Body Angles
_____
_____
_____

Touching

_____
_____
_____

Use of Space (How far apart were the people?)

_____
_____
_____

Paralanguage

Tempo of Speech

_____
_____
_____

Volume of Speech

_____
_____
_____

Number of Pauses

_____
_____
_____

Artifacts (How was each person dressed? What impression did this style of dress leave?)

___

Overall Observation

___

Exercise 11.4
Communication Overload

When employees are overloaded with communication or work, they react in a variety of ways such as error, omission, and escape. Some of these reactions are positive, whereas others are not. It is the purpose of this exercise to provide you with the opportunity to examine the way in which you react when overloaded.

Instructions

Think of the last time when you were highly stressed because you had many things to do but not enough time to get them done.

1) How did you react?

2) Which of the strategies discussed in your text did you use?

3) After reading Chapter 11, what would you do differently?

Exercise 11.5
Your Listening Style

Your text described six listening styles: leisure, inclusive, stylistic, technical, empathic, and nonconforming. To get an idea of your own style, look at the Employee Personality Inventory you took in Exercise 5.4. Your scores on the five personality scales will give you a rough idea of your listening style. The EPI scales and their listening styles are as follows:

EPI Scale	Listening Style
Thinking	Inclusive
Directing	Nonconforming
Communicating	Leisure, Stylistic
Soothing	Empathic
Organizing	Technical

On the basis of your EPI scores, what type of listener are you? Do you agree?

_____
_____
_____
_____
_____
_____
_____
_____
_____
_____
_____
_____
_____
_____

Exercise 11.6
Listening Styles

In your text, you learned that Geier and Downey (1980) believe that there are six styles of listening: leisure, inclusive, stylistic, technical, empathic, and nonconforming. Each style of listener "hears" only communications that are consistent with his/her style. The purpose of this exercise is to provide you with an opportunity to practice communicating in different ways to different types of listeners.

For each of the situations below, indicate how you would speak to each of the six styles of listener.

Situation 1: You are a supervisor and need to tell an employee that his productivity has recently been low and he needs to improve or risk losing his job.

Listening Style	*Your Response*
Leisure	
Inclusive	
Stylistic	
Technical	
Empathic	
Nonconforming	

Situation 2: You are an employee and need to tell your supervisor that you have been working too much overtime and need some time off.

Listening Style	*Your Response*
Leisure	
Inclusive	
Stylistic	
Technical	
Empathic	
Nonconforming	

Exercise 11.7
Listening Quiz

On the following pages, you will find three tests in which you will get the opportunity to rate yourself as a listener. There are no correct or incorrect answers. Your responses, however, will extend your understanding of yourself as a listener. This series of quizzes is provided for you courtesy of UNISYS.

Quiz 1

A. Place a check next to the term that best describes you as a listener.

    ____ Superior
    ____ Excellent
    ____ Above average
    ____ Average
    ____ Below average
    ____ Poor
    ____ Terrible

B. On a scale of 0 to 100 (100 = highest), how would you rate yourself as a listener?

    _____

Quiz 2

How do you think the following people would rate you as a listener? (0-100)

Your best friend _____

Your boss _____

A coworker _____

Your spouse or girl/boyfriend _____

Quiz 3

As a listener, how often do you find yourself engaging in these 10 bad listening habits? First, check the appropriate columns: Almost Always (AA), Usually (U), Sometimes (ST), Seldom (S), or Almost Never (AN). Then tabulate your score using the key below.

Listening habit	AA	U	ST	S	AN
1. Calling the subject uninteresting.					
2. Criticizing the speaker's delivery or mannerisms.					
3. Getting over-stimulated by something the speaker says.					
4. Listening primarily for facts.					
5. Trying to outline everything.					
6. Faking attention to the speaker.					
7. Allowing interfering distractions.					
8. Avoiding difficult material.					
9. Letting emotion-laden words arouse personal antagonism.					
10. Wasting the advantage of thought speed (daydreaming).					

Key: For every "AA" checked, give yourself a score of 2.
For every "U" checked, give yourself a score of 4.
For every "ST" checked, give yourself a score of 6.
For every "S" checked, give yourself a score of 8.
For every "AN" checked, give yourself a score of 10.

TOTAL SCORE _____

PROFILE ANALYSIS

Quiz 1

A. Eighty-five percent of all listeners questioned rated themselves as Average or less. Fewer than 5% rated themselves as Superior or Excellent.

B. On the 0-100 scale, the extreme range is 10-90, the general range is 35-85, and the average rating is 55.

Quiz 2

When comparing the listening self-ratings and projected ratings of others, most respondents believe that their best friend would rate them highest as a listener and that this rating would be higher than the one they gave themselves in Quiz 1.

How come? We can only guess that best friend status is such an intimate, special kind of relationship that you can't imagine it ever happening unless you were a good listener. If you weren't, you and he or she wouldn't be best friends to begin with.

Going down the list, people who take this test usually think their boss would rate them higher than they rated themselves. Now part of that is probably wishful thinking. And part of it is true. We do tend to listen to our bosses better—whether it's out of respect or fear or whatever doesn't matter. The grades for coworker work out to be just the same as the listener rated him/herself—that 55 figure again.

But when you get to your spouse or boy/girlfriend, something really dramatic happens. The score here is significantly lower than the 55 average previous profile takers gave themselves. And what's interesting is that the figure goes steadily downhill. Newlyweds tend to rate their spouse at the same high level as their best friend, but as the marriage goes on, the rating falls. So in a household where the couple has been married 50 years, there could be a lot of talk, but maybe nobody is really listening.

Quiz 3

The average score is a 62 – which is 7 points higher than the average test-taker gave him/herself in Quiz 1. This suggests that when listening is broken down into specific areas of competence, we rate ourselves better than we do when listening is considered only as a generality. Of course, the best way to discover how well you listen is to ask the people to whom you listen most frequently, such as your boss, spouse, and best friend. They'll give you an earful.

Exercise 11.8
Readability

It is important for a piece of writing to be written at a level that can be understood by the people who will read it. This exercise provides you with an opportunity to use the Fry Readability Graph.

Below is a sample of writing. Use the instructions found in your text to count the number of sentences and syllables in the writing sample. Once you have obtained these numbers, use the Fry Readability Graph to determine the readability level of the passage.

It is essential that all employees conduct themselves in a proper fashion, both on and off of company property. Company property includes the factory floor, the lunch room, the parking lot, and all unpaved roads leading to the factory.

Proper conduct entails smiling at customers, not cursing, wearing conservative clothing and bathing daily. If a customer asks a question of an employee, the employee will answer the question to the best of his/her ability. Should the employee not know the answer to the inquiry, he/she will locate another employee who might know the answer to the question. Any employee found to violate any of these essential behaviors will be provided with a warning. Should another violation occur, the employee will be terminated.

Number of total words   _____

Number of sentences   _____

Number of syllables   _____

Sentences per 100 words   _____

Syllables per 100 words   _____

Readability level   _____

Exercise 12.1
Thinking About Leadership

Think of the leader that you respect more than any other leader. This person can be an international, national, or local person. Describe what it is about this person that caused you to choose him/her as your top leader.

_____
_____
_____
_____
_____
_____
_____
_____
_____
_____

Now think of the leader who is your least respected leader. Again, this person can be international, national, or local. What is it about this leader that you do not like?

_____
_____
_____
_____
_____
_____
_____
_____
_____
_____

Exercise 12.2
Understanding Your Leadership Style

The following pages contain four tests of leadership styles that are discussed in this chapter. Before reading any further in the text, follow the instructions for each of the four sections below. After you have completed the tests, continue reading the chapter.

Section A: Answer true or false for the next 18 questions.

1. I find it hard to imitate the behavior of others.   T   F
2. At parties and social gatherings, I do not attempt to do or say things that others will like.   T   F
3. I can only argue for ideas that I already believe.   T   F
4. I can make impromptu speeches even on topics about which I have almost no information.   T   F
5. I guess I put on a show to impress or entertain people.   T   F
6. I would probably make a good actor.   T   F
7. In a group of people, I am rarely the center of attention.   T   F
8. In different situations with different people, I often act like very different people.   T   F
9. I am not particularly good at making other people like me.   T   F
10. I am not always the person I appear to be.   T   F
11. I would not change my opinions in order to please someone else or win their favor.   T   F
12. I have considered being an entertainer.   T   F
13. I have never been good at games like charades or improvisational acting.   T   F
14. I have trouble changing my behavior to suit different people and different situations.   T   F
15. At a party, I let others keep the jokes and stories going.   T   F
16. I feel a bit awkward in company and do not show up quite as well as I should.   T   F
17. I can look anyone in the eye and tell a lie with a straight face (if for the right end).   T   F
18. I may deceive people by being friendly when I really dislike them.   T   F

Section B: Think of the person with whom you can work least well. He/she may be someone you work with now, or he/she may be someone you knew in the past. He/she does not have to be the person you like least well, but should be the person with whom you had the most difficulty in getting a job done. Describe below how this person appears to you by placing a check in the appropriate place on the scale.

Pleasant	__ 8	__ 7	__ 6	__ 5	__ 4	__ 3	__ 2	__ 1	Unpleasant
Friendly	__ 8	__ 7	__ 6	__ 5	__ 4	__ 3	__ 2	__ 1	Unfriendly
Rejecting	__ 1	__ 2	__ 3	__ 4	__ 5	__ 6	__ 7	__ 8	Accepting
Helpful	__ 8	__ 7	__ 6	__ 5	__ 4	__ 3	__ 2	__ 1	Unhelpful
Unenthusiastic	__ 1	__ 2	__ 3	__ 4	__ 5	__ 6	__ 7	__ 8	Enthusiastic
Tense	__ 1	__ 2	__ 3	__ 4	__ 5	__ 6	__ 7	__ 8	Relaxed
Distant	__ 1	__ 2	__ 3	__ 4	__ 5	__ 6	__ 7	__ 8	Close
Cold	__ 1	__ 2	__ 3	__ 4	__ 5	__ 6	__ 7	__ 8	Warm
Cooperative	__ 8	__ 7	__ 6	__ 5	__ 4	__ 3	__ 2	__ 1	Uncooperative
Supportive	__ 8	__ 7	__ 6	__ 5	__ 4	__ 3	__ 2	__ 1	Unsupportive
Boring	__ 1	__ 2	__ 3	__ 4	__ 5	__ 6	__ 7	__ 8	Interesting
Quarrelsome	__ 1	__ 2	__ 3	__ 4	__ 5	__ 6	__ 7	__ 8	Harmonious
Self-assured	__ 8	__ 7	__ 6	__ 5	__ 4	__ 3	__ 2	__ 1	Hesitant
Efficient	__ 8	__ 7	__ 6	__ 5	__ 4	__ 3	__ 2	__ 1	Inefficient
Gloomy	__ 1	__ 2	__ 3	__ 4	__ 5	__ 6	__ 7	__ 8	Cheerful
Open	__ 8	__ 7	__ 6	__ 5	__ 4	__ 3	__ 2	__ 1	Guarded

Section C

For each statement, circle the number corresponding to the extent to which you agree.

SD = strongly disagree
D = disagree
N = neutral
A = agree
SA = strongly agree

		SD	D	N	A	SA
1.	Most employees need to be told what to do.	1	2	3	4	5
2.	Most employees will take advantage of a friendly supervisor.	1	2	3	4	5
3.	Most decisions should be made by management rather than by employees.	1	2	3	4	5
4.	When a supervisor leaves the room, employee effort goes down.	1	2	3	4	5
5.	Most employees who call in sick are probably faking their illness.	1	2	3	4	5
6.	The decline in productivity is mostly due to employees not caring about their work.	1	2	3	4	5
7.	If welfare and work paid the same, few people would choose to work.	1	2	3	4	5

Section D

For each item below, rate the extent to which the statement is true for you. The rating is on a 5-point scale with a rating of 1 indicating that the statement is not at all true of you and a rating of 5 indicating that the statement is very true of you.

	not true at all			very true of me	
1. It is important for me to accomplish many things in life.	1	2	3	4	5
2. It is important for me to have many friends.	1	2	3	4	5
3. I like to be better than others.	1	2	3	4	5
4. I feel hurt when people don't like me.	1	2	3	4	5
5. I always try to get an "A" in every class.	1	2	3	4	5
6. Failure greatly upsets me.	1	2	3	4	5
7. I enjoy being in charge of other people.	1	2	3	4	5
8. I hate to be alone.	1	2	3	4	5
9. Awards are important to me.	1	2	3	4	5
10. I would feel uncomfortable going to a movie alone.	1	2	3	4	5
11. I am much more of a leader than a follower.	1	2	3	4	5
12. It is important for me to be in control.	1	2	3	4	5
13. I need to have close friends.	1	2	3	4	5
14. I hate having people in charge of me.	1	2	3	4	5
15. I have high standards and goals for myself.	1	2	3	4	5

Section E

To give you an idea about your IMPACT leadership styles, go back to Exercise 6-4 and get your scores for the Employee Personality Inventory. Scores on these dimensions roughly correspond with the IMPACT Styles.

EPI Category	Your EPI Score	IMPACT Equivalent
Thinking	_____	Informational
Directing	_____	Position/Coercive
Communicating	_____	Magnetic
Soothing	_____	Affiliation
Organizing	_____	Tactical

Scoring and Interpreting Your Leadership Inventories

Section A

This is the Self-Monitoring Scale. To get your score:

_____ Count the number of times you chose "false" for Questions 1, 2, 3, 7, 9, 11, 13, 14, 15, & 16

_____ Count the number of times you chose "true" for Questions 4, 5, 6, 8, 10, 12, 17, & 18

Add the two numbers to get your self-monitoring score _____.

Section B

This inventory is the Least Preferred Coworker (LPC) Scale. To get your score, add the numbers below each of your checkmarks. For example, your total from the two questions below would be 10 (3 + 7). Your LPC score is _____.

Boring __ __ √__ __ __ __ __ __ Interesting
         1 2 3 4 5 6 7 8

Quarrelsome __ __ __ __ __ __ √__ __ Harmonious
                1 2 3 4 5 6 7 8

Section C

This inventory measures the extent to which you are a task- or person-oriented leader. To score this test, add the points from each of the numbers you circled.

Your task orientation score = _____

Section D

This inventory provides scores on need for achievement, need for affiliation, and need for power. To get your scores, add the numbers you circled for the following questions:

Need for achievement (Questions 1, 5, 6, 9, 15) _____

Need for power (Questions 3, 7, 11, 12, 14) _____

Need for affiliation (Questions 2, 4, 8, 10, 13) _____

Putting it All Together

Transfer your scores from Sections A, B, C, and D onto the chart below.

Leadership Profile

Percentile	Need for Power	Need for Achievement	Need for Affiliation	Self-monitoring	LPC	Task orientation	Percentile
99	24	24	25	17	120	30	99
95	23	23	24	14	103	29	95
90	22		22	13	82	28	90
85	21	22	21	12	77	27	85
80	20		20	11	75	26	80
75	19	21			73		75
70			19	10	71	25	70
65	18				68		65
60		20		9	65	24	60
55	17		18		62		55
50					58		50
45	16		17		56	23	45
40		19		8	55		40
35			16		51	22	35
30	15	18		7	50		30
25			15		46	21	25
20		17	14	6	43	20	20
15	14	16	13	5	40		15
10	13	15	11	4	35	19	10
5	12	14	10	3	27	15	5

_____ _____ _____ _____ _____ _____

Transfer your scores from Section E on the chart below.

IMPACT Leadership Profile

Percentile	Information (Thinking)	Magnetic (Communication)	Position/Coercive (Directing)	Affiliation (Soothing)	Tactical (Organizing)	Percentile
99	14	16	13	16	15	99
95	12	15	11	14	14	95
90	11	14	10	13	13	90
85	10		9	12	12	85
80	9	13	8	11	11	80
75					10	75
70		12	7	10	9	70
65						65
60	8	11		9	8	60
55			6			55
50	7	10		8	7	50
45			5			45
40		9		7		40
35	6	8			6	35
30			4	6		30
25	5	7			5	25
20		6	3	5	4	20
15		5		4		15
10	4	4	2	3	3	10
5	3	3	1	2	2	5

_____   _____   _____   _____   _____

Your Leadership Style

Are you a task- or person-oriented leader? _____

Are you a high- or low-LPC leader? _____

Do you have the leadership motive pattern? _____

Are you a high or low self-monitor? _____

What is your IMPACT style? _____

On the basis of your scores, how would you describe your leadership style? In what situations would you perform best? Worst?

_____

_____

_____

_____

Exercise 13.1
Focused Free-Write

To get you thinking about the relevance of group dynamics in your own life, think of a group that you currently belong to or recently belonged to (e.g., a committee, club, or team). Describe why you joined that group and why you think the group performed as well or as poorly as it did.

Exercise 13.2
Increasing Group Membership

People join groups for a variety of reasons, and a leader who understands this is better able to attract members to the group. To apply what you learned, think of a group you belong to. Why do people join this group? On the basis of the discussion in the chapter, what could you do to attract more members? Be sure to refer back to what you learned in the chapter and to use the terms from the chapter.

Exercise 13.3
Teams

Think of the last team that you were a member of. It could be a work team, an athletic team, or a team assigned to complete a group project. On the basis of what you read in the chapter, answer these questions:

1. Was your team actually a team?

   _____
   _____
   _____
   _____
   _____
   _____
   _____

2. Did the team go through the forming, storming, norming, and performing stages?

   _____
   _____
   _____
   _____
   _____
   _____
   _____

3. Was the team successful? Why or why not?

   _____
   _____
   _____
   _____
   _____
   _____

Exercise 13.4
Competition and Conflict

One of the factors involved in organizational conflict is competition. This exercise will provide you with an opportunity to see how complex conflict can be.

Instructions

First, pair up with another student and read the situation described here. Then individually decide what each of you will do.

Both of you are employees working for separate branches of a national bank. There are seven employees in each branch: a branch manager who manages the branch and recruits new business; a customer service representative who helps customers with loans, IRAs, and special banking problems; a teller supervisor who supervises the tellers; and four tellers.

You are the customer service representative for the Hollow Valley Branch, and your partner is the customer service representative for the Steeple Peak Branch. Both branches are in the same town but usually deal with different customers.

Both of you have heard a rumor that the two branches are going to be merged in a year, that one of the managers will be transferred to another area, and that one of the customer service representatives will be promoted to be the assistant branch manager. You both figure that the customer service representative with the highest volume of loans will be the one promoted. Each of you must make a decision and will not be allowed to talk with the other about this decision. If both of you compete and try to increase the loan volume by going into the other's geographic area, the area manager will be angry and will promote one of the teller supervisors. If neither of you competes and if instead you both try to increase the volume of loans by staying in your own area, the most productive will be promoted and the other will receive a raise. If one of you competes and the other does not, the person who competes will be guaranteed the promotion and the other person will be demoted to teller because his/her loan volume dropped.

Without talking to the other person, decide what you are going to do, and write this choice below.

_____
_____
_____
_____

What did the other person do? If you were the area manager, should you have seen this situation coming? What could you have done to prevent competition?

_____
_____
_____

Exercise 13.5
Cohen Conflict Response Inventory (short version)

Directions: Read the items below and circle the number under the category that indicates how much the item is like you. Answer the questions in terms of how you handle conflict situations. There are no wrong answers to these questions.

		Very unlike me	Unlike me	Neutral	Like me	Very like me
1.	I try to find the best solution to a problem that is acceptable to both parties.	1	2	3	4	5
2.	I try to find a middle-of-the-road solution to conflicts.	1	2	3	4	5
3.	I try to keep myself out of disagreements.	1	2	3	4	5
4.	I usually give-in to other people's needs.	1	2	3	4	5
5.	I tend to use my power or authority to get my way in a conflict situation.	1	2	3	4	5
6.	I share ideas with others so that we may collaborate and develop a final solution.	1	2	3	4	5
7.	I try to find a middle ground solution to a problem.	1	2	3	4	5
8.	I try to avoid argument situations.	1	2	3	4	5
9.	I try to make other people happy.	1	2	3	4	5
10.	I will use threats if I have to in order to get people to see it my way.	1	2	3	4	5
11.	I share resources with others so that we may come up with the best possible solution.	1	2	3	4	5
12.	I try to negotiate with people to find an acceptable solution.	1	2	3	4	5
13.	I tend to avoid engaging in conversations about differences.	1	2	3	4	5
14.	I usually go along with the solutions offered by the other party.	1	2	3	4	5
15.	I often get very angry and hostile when others do not agree to my solution to a problem.	1	2	3	4	5
16.	I try to investigate problems with others s we can get to the root of the problem.	1	2	3	4	5
17.	I try to put all other things aside so that a solution can be reached that is acceptable to all.	1	2	3	4	5
18.	I pretend or deny the fact that a conflict situation exists between myself and another.	1	2	3	4	5
19.	I try to satisfy the needs of others.	1	2	3	4	5
20.	I sometimes bully my way to get others to agree with me.	1	2	3	4	5
21.	I try to meet the needs and goals of both parties to arrive at a final solution.	1	2	3	4	5
22.	I tend to give up some of my own needs arrive at a mutually acceptable decision.	1	2	3	4	5
23.	I usually withdraw from a disagreement.	1	2	3	4	5
24.	I feel it is important to satisfy others' needs.	1	2	3	4	5
25.	I try to show my expertise and knowledge to get others to agree with me.	1	2	3	4	5

Used by permission of the author. Copyright © 1997 by David B. Cohen. All rights reserved.

Scoring: Add the numbers you circled for each statement in each group, and record the total on the blank under Conflict Response Style.

Statement Number and Score	Conflict Response Style
1, 6, 11, 16, and 21	_____ Sage
2, 7, 12, 17, and 22.	_____ Diplomat
3, 8, 13, 18, and 23	_____ Ostrich
4, 9, 14, 19, and 24	_____ Philanthropist
5, 10, 15, 20, and 25	_____ Warrior

The style under which you recorded your highest score is your preferred way of dealing with conflict. Descriptions of the style follow.

Descriptions of Conflict Response Styles

Sage Sages have a high concern for both themselves and the other party involved in a conflict situation. They use an integrating, cooperative conflict style and view conflict in a positive light. This style is solution oriented where an open exchange of information is used. It is associated with problem solving and brainstorming with others that leads to the best possible solution to a conflict. This entails a solution that is mutually beneficial to all parties. Overall, this is the best way to effectively resolve conflict.

Diplomat The Diplomat uses a compromising conflict style. This involves a give and take style to derive a mutually acceptable solution to all parties. Solutions are reached that involve the least amount of personal loss. This occurs from both parties negotiating, splitting the differences, or seeking a middle ground solution to a conflict. Most likely, the end result is not the best solution, but a solution that both parties can live with. Diplomats are concerned with getting their own needs met first.

Ostrich The Ostrich tends to avoid conflict situations at all costs and views conflict in a negative fashion. This style is used to steer clear of conflict situations or to remove oneself from an existing conflict. Ostriches tend to ignore the needs of themselves and others. Sometimes Ostriches will procrastinate when they have to deal with a conflict situation and generally won't deal with it if possible. Most likely they do so because they don't like the stress and tension that conflict creates and feel intimidated by it.

Philanthropist The Philanthropist uses an obliging or peaceful coexistence conflict style. This involves giving up one's own needs to satisfy the needs of others. This style attempts to play down differences and emphasize commonalities to satisfy the concerns of the other party. Philanthropists try to keep other people complacent and will sacrifice their own needs to achieve this. Using this style may send off messages to others that they are pushovers and can be easily persuaded.

Warrior Warriors view conflict as a win-lose situation and will use a dominating, forcing style to get what they want. They view conflict as a positive challenge and an opportunity to win something for themselves. They commonly use threats, aggression, and anger to win. The other party may view Warriors negatively and have resentment and hostility toward them because their focus is so much on themselves that they totally negate the feelings of others.

Do you think this Inventory accurately portrays how you handle conflict? Explain. Which style would you feel least comfortable with?

Exercise 13.6
Reactions to Conflict

The later part of this chapter discussed the types and causes for conflict as well as how people react to conflict. This exercise asks you to apply this material to conflicts you have had in your work experience.

Instructions

Think of the last time you had a conflict with someone at work. Once you have this situation in mind, answer the following questions. Try to use the terms from the text in your answers.

1) What do you think caused the conflict?

   _____
   _____
   _____
   _____
   _____
   _____

2) What type of conflict was it?

   _____
   _____
   _____
   _____

3) How did you react to the conflict?

   _____
   _____
   _____
   _____
   _____

Exercise 13.7
Reacting to Conflicts

The end of this chapter discusses ways in which people react to conflicts. Some of these reactions are beneficial to a person or an organization, but others can be harmful. This exercise provides you with the opportunity to practice these methods and to decide which methods are most appropriate in a given situation.

Instructions

Read the situation below and then write how you would react to the situation if you were using each of the common reactions to conflict.

Joe Hunter has been with the San Angeles Police Department for the past 6 years. After graduating second in his class at the state police academy, Hunter was hired as a patrol person with San Angeles. He quickly moved up in the ranks to corporal in his second year and sergeant in his fourth. All of the officers considered Hunter to be the best cop on the force because of his high level of intelligence as well as his uncanny ability to work with the public by anticipating problems in the community.

Everything was going along well for Sergeant Hunter until the spring of 1988. During this time, he started dating a girl that he quickly fell in love with. What he didn't know until 5 months after they began dating was that she had once been engaged to his captain.

When Hunter's captain discovered the relationship, he was furious with Hunter but knew that legally he could not control the private life of his employees. However, even though he could not directly tell Hunter what to do, he decided to make his life miserable at work. Captain Webb constantly gave Hunter the worst assignments, kept him away from the public contact that made him such a good officer, and started to lower Hunter's performance evaluations.

Hunter was frustrated at first, then hurt, and finally angry. He finally reached a point where one day he was so angry, that he had to do something. If Hunter were to apply each of the common reactions to conflict in this situation, what would he do in each case? Which would be the most appropriate?

Withdrawal

_____
_____
_____
_____
_____
_____

Win at All Costs

_____
_____
_____

Negotiation and Bargaining

Cooperative Problem Solving

Third-Party Interventions

Which of these reactions to conflict do you think would be the most effective in this situation?

Exercise 14.1
Sacred Cow Hunts

For this exercise, get several forms that you must fill out at your university. These can include applications to graduate, registration forms, and change-of-grade forms. For each of the forms, conduct a "paper cow hunt." That is, determine if the form is really needed. If it is, is all the information and are all of the signatures asked for actually necessary?

Form 1:_____

_____

_____

_____

_____

_____

_____

Form 2:_____

_____

_____

_____

_____

_____

_____

Form 3:_____

_____

_____

_____

_____

_____

_____

_____

Exercise 14.2
Acceptance of Change

Think about the last major change you went through either at work or at school. How did you react to the change? What could have made your acceptance of the change better?

_____
_____
_____
_____
_____
_____
_____
_____
_____
_____
_____
_____
_____
_____
_____
_____
_____
_____

Exercise 14.3
Organizational Culture

Think about either your current job or one that you held previously. How would you describe the organizational culture? What types of values, beliefs, and traditions were there? What type of climate existed? Compare this culture to that of another job. If you have not had enough work experience, think about the culture of two classes you have had or about two clubs you have belonged to.

Exercise 14.4
Vroom-Yetton Decision Making Model

The Vroom-Yetton model shown in Figure 14.1 in your text provides leaders with a system to help determine how a decision should be made. This exercise will provide you with the opportunity to use the Vroom-Yetton Model.

Each of these situations requires that a decision be made. Using the chart in Figure 14.1, determine which of the five strategies—Autocratic I, Autocratic II, Consultative I, Consultative II, Group I—the leader should use to make the decision.

Situation A

Jonathon Hancock has been asked to set production goals for his welders and then to return a signed copy of these goals to the plant manager. Mr. Hancock has been a supervisor for 10 years. He always dreads setting goals and does not think they are useful. What strategy should he use?

_____ Autocratic I
_____ Autocratic II
_____ Consultative I
_____ Consultative II
_____ Group I

Why did you choose this strategy?

_____

_____

_____

Situation B

Krista Harrison is the branch manager for a small bank and must schedule vacations for her 10 employees. The regional manager wants the vacation list in the next week. What strategy should she use?

_____ Autocratic I
_____ Autocratic II
_____ Consultative I
_____ Consultatve II
_____ Group I

Why did you choose this strategy?

_____

_____

_____

Situation C

Kent Clark is an optometrist and has four assistants working for him. Dr. Clark is considering purchasing a new piece of equipment that will allow him to more accurately measure the vision needs of his patients. What decision-making strategy should he use?

____ Autocratic I
____ Autocratic II
____ Consultative I
____ Consultatve II
____ Group I

Why did you choose this strategy?

_____
_____
_____
_____
_____

Situation D

Debika Johnson is the vice-president for Reilly College. She has been at Reilly for 6 months and must create a policy for student evaluation of faculty. That is, she needs to decide what type of evaluation instrument will be used, how often evaluations will occur, and how much weight the student evaluations should carry in the overall evaluation of a faculty member. What stratefy should she use?

____ Autocratic I
____ Autocratic II
____ Consultative I
____ Consultatve II
____ Group I

Why did you choose this strategy?

_____
_____
_____
_____
_____

Exercise 14.5
Downsizing

On the basis of the chapter's discussion of downsizing, develop the ideal downsizing program. How would you announce the downsizing? What types of services would you offer victims, survivors, and the community?

Exercise 14.6
Work Schedules

Instructions

Read the situation described below and then use your knowledge of work schedules to create a state-of-the-art scheduling program for the organization.

The computer services department at Taflinger University consists of 38 employees in several divisions. The administrative division consists of a vice president for computer services, a director of administration, two administrative assistants, a receptionist, and two student workers. It is the job of the administration division to administer the computing center and to coordinate all computing activities in the university. Currently, the administrative division is open from 8:00 a.m. to 5:00 p.m., Monday through Friday, and has constant contact with the other departments in the university.

The programming division employs a director of programming, six programmers, three programmer/analysts, and one student worker. The function of the programming division is to write the programs needed to operate the university. For example, they write and update programs for the registrar's office and the payroll office. Employees in this division have occasional contact with employees in other departments.

The computer operations division consists of a director of operations, six computer operators, one tape librarian, two technicians, two clerks, and two student workers. This division is in operation 24 hours a day, 7 days a week. With the exception of the two technicians, none of the employees has contact with people outside of the computing center. Even though they are scheduled from 8:00 a.m. to 5:00 p.m., the technicians are basically "on call" and work whenever computing equipment needs to be fixed.

The academic computing division is staffed by a director for academic computing, two full-time lab assistants, and three part-time student workers. It is the job of this division to serve the computing needs of the various academic departments by operating the student computer lab, helping professors with computer problems, and recommending academic software to be purchased.

Given this wide range of jobs and duties, how would you design a work schedule?

_____

_____

_____

_____

_____

_____

_____

_____

_____

Exercise 14.1
Type A Behavior

Instructions: If you are a Type A person, indicate the extent to which you agree with each statement by using a scale:

5 – Agree
4 – Somewhat agree
3 – Neutral
2 – Somewhat disagree
1 – Disagree

1. I work fast and I don't have plenty of time to get things done.
2. I'm anxious to be important.
3. I do things.
4. I eat fast while I am doing other things such as reading or watching TV.
5. Close friends or relatives tell me to slow down and take it easy or to not work so devilishly together.
6. I get irritated when I struggle and try to finish one as it goes.
7. I get impatient in regards to the work I must do.
8. I walk and/or speak slowly in it, etc.
9. When I have my mind set on certain tasks, I am easily distracted.
10. When having a conversation about a topic I am interested in, I often dominate the conversation.
11. I keep all of my school notes as orderly as possible.
12. I relax when others are in control of a situation I am in.
13. I expect the highest grade in my class on any given project.
14. On days when I have completed my homework, I have a difficult time sleeping.
15. When I make a mistake and correct it, I view the experience as a learning experience and don't get upset.

162

Exercise 15.1
Type A Behavior

To determine if you are a Type A personality, complete the Gardner Personality Test below. Circle the number that corresponds to the extent to which you never, rarely, sometimes, usually, or always engage in each of these behaviors.

N = Never
R = Rarely
S = Sometimes
U = Usually
A = Always

		N	R	S	U	A
1.	I walk fast even when I have plenty of time to get where I am going.	1	2	3	4	5
2.	I am on time for appointments.	1	2	3	4	5
3.	I daydream.	5	4	3	2	1
4.	I eat a meal while I am doing other things such as studying or watching TV.	1	2	3	4	5
5.	Close friends or relatives tell me to slow down and take it easier when we participate in activities together.	1	2	3	4	5
6.	I complete school assignments in as little time as possible.	1	2	3	4	5
7.	I must attain all my goals in the time frame I set.	1	2	3	4	5
8.	People who speak slowly irritate me.	1	2	3	4	5
9.	When I have my mind set on certain tasks, I am easily distracted.	5	4	3	2	1
10.	When having a conversation about a topic I am interested in, I let others dominate the conversation.	5	4	3	2	1
11.	I keep all of my school notes as orderly as possible.	1	2	3	4	5
12.	I relax when others are in control of a situation I am in.	5	4	3	2	1
13.	I expect the highest grade in my class on any given project.	1	2	3	4	5
14.	On days when I have completed my homework, I have a difficult time relaxing.	1	2	3	4	5
15.	When I make a mistake and correct it, I view the experience as a learning experience and don't get upset.	5	4	3	2	1

To get your Type A score, add the numbers you circled for each item. Your score is _____.
The higher your score, the more likely you are to be a Type A personality.

Your Type A Score	Percentile
69 - 75	99
62 - 68	95
60 - 61	90
55 - 59	80
53 - 54	70
50 - 52	60
48 - 49	50
46 - 47	40
44 - 45	30
42 - 43	20
37 - 41	10
00 - 36	5

What does your score say about your personality?

_____
_____
_____
_____
_____
_____
_____
_____
_____
_____
_____

Exercise 15.2
Optimism

For each of the questions below, indicate the extent to which you agree or disagree with the statement.

SD = Strongly disagree
D = Disagree
N = Neutral
A = Agree
SA = Strongly agree

		SD	D	N	A	SA
1.	I try to learn from my failures	1	2	3	4	5
2.	Most people are good	1	2	3	4	5
3.	If something can go wrong, it will	5	4	3	2	1
4.	I can handle most of life's difficulties	1	2	3	4	5
5.	It is difficult to trust people	5	4	3	2	1
6.	I enjoy life.	1	2	3	4	5
7.	One can find something positive in most bad situations.	1	2	3	4	5
8.	I have a great life ahead of me.	1	2	3	4	5
9.	I find it hard to find things I enjoy doing.	5	4	3	2	1
10.	Life is hard.	5	4	3	2	1
11.	I will be very successful in my career.	1	2	3	4	5
12.	Most people who meet me will like me.	1	2	3	4	5
13.	Most politicians are crooks and liars.	5	4	3	2	1
14.	Most people will help you if they can.	1	2	3	4	5
15.	Most people would say I have a good attitude.	1	2	3	4	5
16.	I am usually happy.	1	2	3	4	5
17.	I feel that I control my own destiny.	1	2	3	4	5
18.	I make other people happy.	1	2	3	4	5
19.	I seldom complain.	1	2	3	4	5
20.	I often seem to focus too much on the negative aspects of life.	5	4	3	2	1
21.	There are few problems that can't be solved.	1	2	3	4	5
22.	Life just seems so boring.	5	4	3	2	1
23.	People who want to be successful can be successful.	1	2	3	4	5
24.	I can smile in even the worst of situations.	1	2	3	4	5

To get your Optimism score, add the numbers you circled for each item. Your score is _____.
High scores indicate you are an optimist, whereas lower scores indicate you are a pessimist.
Pessimists are more likely to be affected by stress.

Your Optimism Score	Percentile
107 - 120	99
105 - 106	95
102 - 104	90
99 - 101	80
95 - 98	70
93 - 94	60
90 - 92	50
87 - 89	40
84 - 86	30
81 - 83	20
79 - 80	10
24 - 78	5

What does this score say about your stress-related personality?

_____
_____
_____
_____
_____
_____
_____
_____
_____
_____

Exercise 15.3
Lifestyle Questionnaire

Circle the number on the right that best corresponds to your answer for each of these 10 questions.

1. How many cigarettes do you smoke each day?   1 2 3 4 5
   1 = none, 2 = a few cigarettes, 3 = half a pack, 4 = one pack, 5 = more than one pack

2. How often do you drink alcohol?   1 2 3 4 5
   1 = never, 2 = once a month 3 = once a week,
   4 = 2 to 3 times a week, 5 = more than 3 times a week

3. How often do you drink beverages with caffeine?   1 2 3 4 5
   1 = never, 2 = once a month, 3 = once or twice a week
   4 = 3 to 5 times a week, 5 = more than 5 times a week

4. How often do you eat fruit?   1 2 3 4 5
   5 = never, 4 = once a month, 3 = once a week, 2 = several times a week, 1 = daily

5. How often do you eat vegetables?   1 2 3 4 5
   5 = never, 4 = once a month, 3 = once a week, 2 = several times a week, 1 = daily

6. How often do you exercise or play sports?   1 2 3 4 5
   5 = never, 4 = once a month, 3 = once a week, 2 = several times a week, 1 = daily

7. How many glasses of water do you drink on a normal day?   1 2 3 4 5
   5 = none, 4 = one, 3 = two, 2 = three or four, 1 = five or more

8. How many hours of sleep do you normally get each night?   1 2 3 4 5
   1 = more than eight, 2 = eight, 3 = seven, 4 = six, 5 = less than six

9. How many times in a week do you take a short nap?   1 2 3 4 5
   1 = five or more, 2 = four, 3 = three, 4 = one or two, 5 = none

10. How cluttered is the room, house, or office where you spend most of your time?   1 2 3 4 5
    1 = very neat, 2 = neat, 3 = average, 4 = cluttered, 5 = very cluttered

To get your Lifestyle score, add the numbers you circled for each item. Your score is _____.
The higher the score, the more your lifestyle makes you susceptible to the effects of stress.

Your Lifestyle Score	Percentile
35 - 50	99
33 - 34	95
32	90
30 - 31	80
29	70
27 - 28	60
26	50
25	40
24	30
23	20
21 - 22	10
10 - 20	5

On the basis of your score, what lifestyle changes can you make to make you less susceptible to the effects of stress?

_____
_____
_____
_____
_____
_____
_____
_____
_____
_____

Exercise 15.4
Empowering and Motivating Yourself:
Gaining Control Over Your Life

1. List those areas in your life over which you want to gain more control. These areas could be in your working situation, personal life, or both. Be sure to write down only those areas you believe you can control *(e.g., "More control over where my money goes and how much money I have")*.

   _____
   _____
   _____
   _____
   _____
   _____
   _____

2. Now, for each area you listed above, write down specific steps you are going to take to get better control. If you aren't sure how to do it, talk with a classmate, friend, or family member for suggestions and ideas. Be specific about how you will empower yourself *(e.g., Write down a daily budget; stay within that budget; get a job or ask for a raise; put money into savings account)*.

   _____
   _____
   _____
   _____
   _____
   _____
   _____
   _____
   _____

3. Finally, write down those items you want to control but feel you can't. Discuss them with someone you trust. Can you think of ways to take more control (if not complete control) in those areas? If so, using these new items, do Question 2 again.

   _____
   _____
   _____
   _____
   _____